Why?

Thinking About Plane Crashes

Peter Garrison

See page 239 for Glossary !

Foreword

In 1980 I took over Flying Magazine's "Aftermath" column , which until 1977 had been called "Pilot Error". I have written it almost every month for the past 40 years.

In general, the facts presented in Aftermath are those that I find in the National Transportation Safety Board's report on the accident, though I occasionally add some circumstantial details drawn from newspaper accounts and obituaries.

Readers who are curious to see the raw material of these commentaries can find the NTSB's accident reports online, chronologically arranged, at https://www.ntsb.gov/_layouts/ ntsb.aviation/month.aspx. Reports emerge in a series of stages culminating in the Final Report, which includes the NTSB's finding of "probable cause." The site includes a database query page that allows you to search for accidents by location, type of aircraft, and so on, and also by the presence of words or phrases in the final report.

Not all NTSB reports are created equal. Some are quite perfunctory, others detailed and probing. Ones involving well-known people and passenger-filled airliners get a more thorough treatment than the lonely fall of a single-engine plane with a single private pilot aboard. It is to the prominent accidents that the NTSB's top investigative talent is dispatched; the obscure ones are delegated to local FAA employees.

The purpose of Flying's Aftermath column is not to gloat over the misfortunes and blunders of others, though these sometimes have a certain undeniable fascination. It is to learn to recognize patterns of behavior and thinking that lead to accidents. My qualification for writing these columns is that there, but for better luck, go I. I started flying at 18, and am still flying at 76. Having experienced in the air the arrogant folly of youth and the forgetfulness and ineptitude of age, and many forms of negligence and stupidity that go between, I empathize with the pilots about whom I write. I hope readers will as well.

Although I have lightly edited some of these essays, I have not changed time references. Thus, words like "recently" and "ago" refer to the time when the piece first appeared, not to the present.

Peter Garrison
Los Angeles, 2020

Contents

I Can Swim, Leander Said

It's an old story. As old as the Greeks, in fact, though it has been retold many times and in many versions. Its erotic, pathetic, heroic and cautionary elements receive different emphases from authors with different axes to grind. In brief, Leander was a youth who lived on one shore of the Hellespont, the narrow strait that separates Greece from Asia Minor. He became the lover of a priestess of Aphrodite — her name was Hero, pronounced more like hair-oh — who dwelt on the other shore. He would visit her nightly, swimming across the channel while she set out a lantern to guide him. One night it was stormy, and Leander drowned.

The worldly-wise Lord Byron once swam the Hellespont in Leander's honor. He later complained that, while the brave Greek youth won eternal fame, all he got for his pains was a cold.

What moral should we draw from the story of Leander? That love cannot, in fact, conquer all? That youthful rashness and rough water go ill together? Perhaps something more general, about recklessness and any sort of dangerous activity.

A 21-year-old Alabama man began taking flying lessons on October 30. He got his student certificate a week later, at that point reporting six hours of flight experience. In his application for the third class medical, he did not mention that he had used a prescription antidepressant when he was 18, and had then been treated with a series of other medications for a diagnosis of "attention deficit hyperactivity disorder," a recently discovered ailment mainly of disruptive or unfocused schoolboys. For the past few months he had been taking daily doses of Adderall, an amphetamine "study drug" that has the paradoxical property of stimulating the enervated while calming the agitated.

The student pilot pursued his flying lessons assiduously. He made his first solo flight in the pattern on December 20 and his second on the 23rd. An instructor endorsed his logbook for solo flying within 25 miles of the home airport, with limitations: daytime only, no passengers, wind not to exceed 10 knots, maximum crosswind component six knots, ceiling above 2,300 feet, and visibility no less than six miles. The instructor also explained these limitations to him personally.

At this point he had logged 26 hours, a quarter of them at night. He had not yet received any cross-country instruction.

On December 23, the student pilot bought himself a 37-year-old, recently inspected Cherokee 140.

The evening of December 24 was forecast to be stormy, with wind and rain. An instructor, observing the student fueling his newly-acquired airplane a little after noon, told him that he "needed to be through flying for the day" because of the weather. The student agreed and said that he would put the plane away.

At 2:50, the airport security camera recorded the pilot returning, and about five minutes later an airplane that appeared to be his taxied to the runway. The security camera caught no more comings or goings of the pilot or his airplane, but it did note the pilot-controlled runway lights going on at 9:58 p.m.

The student pilot had been planning to visit his girlfriend at her parents' in Atlanta the following day, Christmas, but he decided to fly to Atlanta that night instead. He spoke with her between 8:45 and 9:45. She tried to dissuade him. She told him that the weather was bad and that it was raining hard. There was a high wind advisory for the area.

He replied, "I'm a pilot."

He said he would land at 11:30. When he had not arrived by two in the morning, his girlfriend called the authorities. The next afternoon the wreckage of the Cherokee was located in a national forest 35 miles east of the departure airport. There was no wreckage path; the engine buried in the ground, the symmetrical crushing of both wings, and the lack of damage to the tail cone and empennage and to the surrounding trees indicated that the airplane had come down in a vertical dive, probably having stalled and spun. Investigators found nothing to suggest a pre-impact failure of the engine or flight controls.

The weather at the departure airport on the evening of the flight had been windy but VFR, with five- or six-mile visibility, an overcast at around 3,000 feet, and gusts to 20 knots. At Atlanta, there were 30-knot gusts, but the visibility and ceiling were better. At Anniston, Alabama, the weather reporting station closest to the accident site, the wind was gusting to 25 and the visibility occasionally dropping below three miles in rain and mist. There was no evidence, however, that the pilot had sought a weather briefing from any of the usual augurs.

The accident occurred in a hilly area where, with the strong east wind blowing, terrain-induced rain and fog were probable. Witnesses from the vicinity of the accident site reported heavy rain and high winds. A fire department officer at Anniston had received numerous calls regarding blown-down power lines.

The autopsy of the pilot found residues of amphetamines and alcohol in his blood and tissues. Investigators obtained pharmacy records that revealed that his most recent Adderall prescription had been filled the day before the accident. Five of the pills were already gone, implying that the young man had been taking them at twice the prescribed rate. Detritus recovered from the wreckage suggested, without however confirming it, a minor orgy of self-medication: an emptied can of Red Bull energy drink, an ashtray full of cigarette butts, a water bottle containing chewed tobacco, four unopened cans of beer in a duffel, and four other beer cans, scattered about, which were too badly damaged for it to be determined whether or not they had been opened.

Despite the fact that the student pilot had only just soloed and was not authorized to carry passengers, his girlfriend told investigators that she had flown with him several times. She described him as a good pilot who could fly in instrument conditions and "with or without the GPS." He was, however, "hard-headed." His flight instructor supplied a slightly less flattering account, saying that he was "pretty good" at night flying and "terrible" on instruments. He was "overconfident," and his buying himself an airplane had perhaps magnified his "attitude that he could do anything." His driving record suggested a protracted, but perhaps not untypical, male adolescence: three speeding tickets, and one for running a red light; two accidents, fault unspecified; and a 60-day license suspension for "mutilating, defacing or reproducing" a driver's license.

6

From a certain point of view, some amount of irrational optimism might be seen as useful for a pilot. After all, he expects to be suspended aloft, like a saint or a character in a martial arts film, by invisible forces. Certainly the earliest pilots were, for the most part, a daring, devil-may-care lot, for whom ordinary life was, as a poet wrote of a First World War airman, "a waste of breath / In balance with this life, this death." But times have changed. The chief virtue of a pilot is no longer reckless courage; it is cautious good judgment.

By any measure, the young man's decision to fly that night was a reckless one — wildly, rashly, irretrievably reckless. One senses in him — to the extent that one can sense anything through the obscure prism of a government accident report — a judgment buffeted between tempestuous impulses and the medicines that were supposed to regulate them. Can such a judgment fairly balance the urge to make a flight and the conditions that militate against it? Can it even be relied upon to see the need for balancing them? This novice pilot seems, once he made up his mind, not to have considered any alternative. The advice and warnings of his instructor, the admonitory notations in his logbook, might as well have been incised on a buried cuneiform tablet. They were not part of his mental world. It was not so much his disregard of the regulations that doomed him; it was his disregard of the *sense* of the regulations.

In fairness to the young pilot, it should be said that this kind of accident is not uncommon. It is by no means confined to amorous youths with ADHD and a student ticket. Licensed pilots with neither instrument training nor suitable equipment regularly take off in darkness, fog and rain, only to hit a tree or a hillside within a few miles of the airport. It is difficult to imagine what they were thinking. But perhaps there is some underlying sense of a glory in facing terrible odds. The grand gesture, ending badly, looks like folly to a modern eye. But think of Leander. If he had stayed home that night, we would never have heard of him.

Ace of the Base

In *Testing Time*, her anecdote-rich account of the history of British test flying, Constance Babington Smith quotes a memo written by Jeffrey Quill, then Supermarine's chief test pilot, to a subordinate.

"I have no complaints," Quill wrote, "about your actual test work but I consider you handle an aircraft in far too slapdash a fashion — your aerobatic manoeuvres and turns are all sharp and sudden and there is no smoothness or finesse in them, and I can always recognize your takeoffs by the violent way in which you handle the engine controls after leaving the ground.

"I have a feeling that you think this method of flying appears more impressive from the ground, but I can assure you you are wrong ... I want you to get out of the habit of handling a Spitfire in the way that young boys drive M.G. Midgets on the Brighton Road on a Sunday afternoon. It is a cheap way of flying and you will do yourself harm by it because no one will take you seriously."

The impulse to grandstand is not rare among pilots — least so, perhaps, among military ones. It would be an exaggeration to say that ego and airplanes shouldn't mix — they can and do, sometimes to the benefit of both — but at the same time Quill's reference to boy racers on the Brighton Road evokes the sense of immaturity conveyed when a pilot tries to show off. Egotistical self-indulgence can be harmless or extremely dangerous, depending on the circumstances.

It's been almost a dozen years now since a B-52 crashed at Fairchild Air Force Base, in Spokane, Washington, while practicing for an airshow. The accident, which killed four field-grade Air Force officers, was captured on an amateur videotape that, being horrific, now circulates widely on the Internet. It has become an oft-cited example of what could be called the "ace of the base syndrome" — a complex of reciprocal relationships between a pilot, his superiors and his subordinates that is pregnant, as the eventual crash demonstrated, with the potential for disaster.

The year after the accident, Air Force Major Anthony Kern, working independently of the official crash investigation, produced a well-documented study of the events leading up to it. Entitled "Darker Shades of Blue" and, like the accident video, readily obtainable on the Internet, Kern's study examines the relationships surrounding Lt. Col. Bud Holland, the pilot of the ill-fated B-52, from a management perspective, attempting to identify the dynamics that shielded him from administrative action from above while, at the same time, making him an object of both fear and admiration among his subordinates.

Colonel Holland was, ironically, chief of Fairchild's Standardization and Evaluation Section — in other words, he was the main quality-control guy for the pilots in his bomber wing. He was charismatic and, by general consent, a "singularly outstanding 'stick and rudder pilot'" and B-52 driver without peer; but he was also a scofflaw who systematically placed himself outside the pale of regulations. Some of his fellow pilots absolutely would not fly with him. No one was surprised when he crashed. "You could see it, hear it, feel it, and smell it coming," said one B-52 crewmember. "We were all just trying to be somewhere else when it happened."

It happened on June 24, 1994. Holland's airplane was returning to land after rehearsing maneuvers for an upcoming airshow — maneuvers which "grossly exceeded aircraft and regulatory limitations," and which had not received the approval of the Wing Commander, despite Holland's reputation as a magician in the B-52. Another airplane was on the runway, and Holland had to go around. The gear and flaps were down. At midfield Holland racked the bomber around in a tight turn at an

altitude of 250 feet — its wingspan is 185 feet — with a
bank angle that was almost vertical. About halfway
around the turn, the bomber's nose began to drop.
Holland tried to roll out — in the video the spoilers can
be seen emerging from the right wing as the airplane
turns toward the camera — but there was neither enough
roll authority nor enough time. The nose continued to arc
downward. The left wing struck a power line and then
the ground, and the bomber vanished in a maelstrom of
black smoke and orange flame.

It's worth pausing for a moment to consider why, in
aerodynamic terms, this accident happened. Holland was
no stranger to unusual attitudes in the B-52. He was the
go-to guy for airshows, and would regularly pull up to a
60-degree climb and then recover with a wingover turn
— both maneuvers that are forbidden in the B-52, which
is neither a particularly strong airplane nor a particularly
agile one. He had also previously performed steep turns,
in excess of 60 degrees of bank, with flaps down, close to
the ground. Why did this turn get away from him? He
may, for one thing, have felt that he had something to
prove to the right-seat pilot, who had tried to have him
grounded. In any case, the bank angle this time was far
more than 60 degrees. Holland may have found the
airplane losing energy more rapidly than he expected,
and not realized that as the nose yawed downward, the
dihedral effect of the swept wings would counteract his
efforts to roll out.

12

Lt. Col. Holland's "considerable social skills" and the grudging admiration that his stunts inspired insulated him and allowed him to "bend [his superior officers] to his will." Major Kern's monograph revisits Holland's previous airshow performances to document a pattern of blatant rule-breaking that was quietly tolerated by higher-ups. In 1991, at another Fairchild AFB airshow, and later that same year at a change of command flyover, Holland exceeded aircraft bank and pitch limits and flew at low altitude directly over the crowd. No one complained because, as one pilot later put it, "What was the sense in saying anything? They had already given him a license to steal." After the second incident, however, concerned that Holland's flying style was creating a "perception problem with the young aircrews" — namely, they perceived that rules were not to be taken seriously — his superiors "debriefed and verbally reprimanded" him.

With little effect. At the next Fairchild airshow, in 1992, Holland repeated his habitual excesses, and again in 1993. By this time "younger, less skilled crewmembers" were actually trying to emulate Holland's maneuvers; one nearly stalled a B-52 during an attempted wingover (the maneuver is explicitly forbidden because it can overstress the airframe), and another received an administrative reprimand and was grounded. Yet Holland himself continued to be respected as "totally professional."

In 1994, three months before the fatal accident, Holland's B-52 participated in a simulated bombing mission for the benefit of a photographer on the ground. An instructor pilot in the right seat found himself staring at an approaching ridge. "I didn't see any clearance ... it appeared to me that he had target fixation. I said 'Climb — climb — climb.' He did not do it. I grabbed a hold of the yoke and I pulled it back pretty abruptly ... I'd estimate we had a cross over about 15 feet ... The radar navigator and the navigator were ... yelling [and] screaming .. [Holland's] reaction ... was he was laughing — I mean a good belly laugh."

The next day the right-seat pilot reported to the operations officer that "I did not ever want to fly with Lt. Col. Holland again, even if it meant that I could not fly any more as an Air Force pilot." The ops officer replied that it wouldn't come to that because "he was joining a group of pilots in the squadron who had also made the same statement."

Now began a chain of events that would have tragic consequences. The ops officer went to the Squadron Commander, Lt. Col. Mark McGeehan. They agreed that Holland needed to be grounded for his own and others' safety, and went to the Deputy Commander for Operations (DO) with that recommendation. The DO, however, having heard Holland's side of the story, declined to put any restriction on his flying. McGeehan then declared that he would not allow any of his crews to fly with Holland unless he himself were in the right seat. It was a fateful decision.

By now the controversy surrounding Holland was familiar to everyone on the base, including aircrews' families, and possibly even to the surrounding civilian community. According to one instructor pilot, "Everyone had a Col. Holland scare story ... the hypocrisy was amazing. For him to be in [his] position ... [was] unconscionable ... What's the crew force supposed to learn from that? You got the 'He's about to retire' [and] ' ... he has more hours in the B-52 than you do sleeping.' Yeah, he might have that many hours, but he became complacent, reckless, and willfully violated regulations."

Notwithstanding the widespread uneasiness among his colleagues, Holland was selected to fly the B-52 in what was to be his last airshow. And, despite the hostility between him and Lt. Col. Holland, Mark McGeehan, true to his word, took the right seat and died with him.

As aberrant as this story seems, it is neither unique nor psychologically implausible. Nor are the patterns that it reveals confined to the military environment. They can materialize anywhere. The combination of skill and daring commands respect. The fact that risk-taking behavior can continue for a long time without mishap makes it appear less dangerous; what's more, it appears that it is safe precisely because of the skill of the risk-taker. The talented and daring pilot makes himself the exception to the rules everyone else is expected to follow. It's difficult, particularly in certain kinds of competitive, often largely male environments, to object to risk-taking behavior, because too slavish a respect for the rulebook appears weak and fussy.

Major Kern ends his essay with the observation that a good many young aviators who "grew up" with Lt. Col. Holland as their role model are still flying in the Air Force and "passing along what they ... learned." Therefore, he rather gloomily concludes, "the final domino in this chain of events may not yet have fallen." But that can be true only if those pilots fail to see the connection between Holland's end and all that went before.

Kennedy

When I was a kid there was a TV series called *You Are There* that consisted of hokey re-enactments of historical events. It closed with the voice of Walter Cronkite intoning, "It was a day like all days, filled with those events that alter and illuminate our times."

That sentence stuck in my mind as a persistent riddle. Did it mean that historic events come so fast and furious that every day is full of them? Or did it mean that even commonplace events "alter and illuminate" history? Or was it perhaps just a sonorous phrase, signifying nothing?

In the 1950s you could wonder about things like that. Today the answer is obvious. Commonplace events are historic when they involve celebrities.

The National Transportation Safety Board's report on the accident that killed John F. Kennedy Jr. last summer is 35 pages long — about ten times as long as the typical report on an accident of this kind. It is extremely rich in detail about the few things that can be known — for example, the exact manner in which various pieces of the wreckage of Kennedy's Piper Saratoga were bent and broken. It is couched in the usual professional accident-investigator's language, but with an occasional nod to the lay reader, as when, in the midst of thickets of technical jargon, the word "transponder" is suddenly defined. Like all accident narratives it carefully avoids ungrounded speculation about the course of events leading to the crash; but on the other hand it lays out various bits of information that nudge the reader toward, if not a conclusion, at least a suspicion. The finding of probable cause will surprise no one:

The pilot's failure to maintain control of the airplane during a descent over water at night, which was a result of spatial disorientation. Factors in the accident were haze, and the dark night.

This is pretty much what everyone thought the day after the accident. In July, 1999, most commentators in the media presented Kennedy as an inexperienced pilot, under-qualified and over-equipped, who had got in over his head. Some suggested that a kind of spoiled-child bravado, endemic to his jet-setting ilk, had driven Kennedy to launch into weather that was beyond his capabilities. At the time, this was pure storytelling; no one knew whether the accident had been due to pilot error, incapacitation, autopilot, instrument or engine failure, or perhaps — given the location — even a stray missile from a Navy ship.

The spin is different now. To begin with, Kennedy was not under-qualified. He had logged about 310 hours, 55 of them at night (these figures, which are estimated because his most recent logbook was lost, do not include simulator training). He had flown the route of the accident flight 35 times in the past 15 months, five times at night. He was halfway through the training for the instrument rating, and had passed the written test. He had received a great deal of flight instruction, and it seems to have been of high quality. Instructors and examiners characterized him as an average to above-average pilot.

It's true that Kennedy's airplane was extremely well equipped, with two-axis autopilot, flight director, coupled GPS, moving-map display, dual vacuum systems, and so on. But the Saratoga itself is hardly the airborne Ferrari that some reporters depicted — perhaps they were misled by the stock FAA phrase "high performance aircraft," which includes everything from a 182 on up — and its elaborate avionics would have made a night flight over water simpler, not more difficult. The airplane was well maintained, and the engine had been overhauled about a year and 280 flight hours before the accident.

One notable peculiarity of Kennedy's career as a private pilot was the vast amount of dual instruction he had received; of his 310 hours, only around 72 — including the five night trips to Martha's Vineyard — had been flown without a CFI aboard.

There was nothing rash about Kennedy's setting out that night for Martha's Vineyard, 170 nm distant. The skies were generally clear and, although there were forecasts of haze, visibilities were at least three to four miles everywhere in the vicinity and in most places more than that. There were no clouds, no precipitation, nothing that would give a 300-hour pilot a moment's pause. One pilot, who had told the news media that he had decided not to fly that night because of the weather, later explained to the NTSB that his reasons for delaying his departure until the next morning had had as much to do with the failure of some expected passengers to show up and the cost of a hotel room on the Vineyard.

It's true — although Kennedy could not have known it when he took off — that there were areas of reduced visibility in haze over the water. The pilot of a twin turboprop flying from Teterboro to Nantucket looked down when he was passing over Martha's Vineyard and saw nothing; he thought there might have been a power failure on the island. Another pilot, flying from Bar Harbor, Maine, to Long Island, estimated that the visibility between Cape Cod and Long Island was only two to three miles at 6,000 feet. On the other hand, the tower operator at Vineyard Haven (MVN) thought that at the time of the accident the visibility was probably a little better than the eight miles being reported by the airport's automated weather-observing system. Arriving pilots had reported the airport in sight when they were still 10 to 12 miles out, and the tower operator had been able to see their lights. That Kennedy encountered an area of semi-opaque haze near Martha's Vineyard is only a hypothesis.

Although Kennedy had no radio contact with ground stations after his takeoff from Essex County airport in New Jersey, the track of the flight was reconstructed from radar records. As was reported in the news media at the time, he flew a 100-degree course away from the New York area, paralleling the Connecticut and Rhode Island coasts before heading out over the Rhode Island Sound at the western edge of Narragansett Bay. The distance from that point to Gay Head, the western extremity of Martha's Vineyard, is less than 30 nautical miles, and most of the course lies only seven or eight miles from the populous and well-lighted Massachusetts coastline.

Up to that point, the Saratoga had been cruising at 5,500 feet. Shortly after leaving the shoreline at Point Judith, it began to descend at between 400 and 800 feet per minute. It continued to track toward MVN, probably making a good 180 knots over the ground. A 400-fpm descent would have put it at pattern altitude when it reached the airport.

In the vicinity of the floating radio beacon labeled "BUZZARD BAY ENT" on VFR charts, the airplane began a turn to the right. Here is the NTSB's description of the flight path as recorded by ATC radar:

"About 2138, the target began a right turn in a southerly direction. About 30 seconds later, the target stopped its descent at 2,200 feet and began a climb that lasted another 30 seconds. During this period of time, the target stopped the turn, and the airspeed decreased [from 160 kias] to about 153 kias. About 2139, the target leveled off at 2,500 feet and flew in a southeasterly direction. About 50 seconds later, the target entered a left turn and climbed to 2,600 feet. As the target continued in the left turn, it began a descent that reached a rate of about 900 fpm. When the target reached an easterly direction, it stopped turning; its rate of descent remained about 900 fpm. At 2140:15, while still in the descent, the target entered a right turn. As the target's turn rate increased, its descent rate and airspeed also increased. The target's descent rate eventually exceeded 4,700 fpm. The target's last radar position was recorded at 2140:34 at an altitude of 1,100 feet."

The airplane apparently struck the water in a semi-inverted dive, right wing first. This is an attitude that could not result from a graveyard spiral; it can only be the result of pilot commands. Much of the severely fragmented wreckage was recovered from 120 feet below the surface, but, as far as investigators could determine, there was no evidence of airframe, control system, engine or equipment failure prior to impact.

They were able to obtain some instrument and control settings. Marks on the face of the attitude indicator suggested 125 degrees of bank, that is, 35 degrees past wings-vertical. Both tach and manifold pressure readings were at the maximum: 27 inches and 2700 rpm. The fuel flow reading of 22 gph was consistent with those figures, but the position of the fuel selector handle — OFF — was not. The autopilot was turned off. The GPS settings were lost; but frequencies were recovered from the nonvolatile memory of the navcoms. Two had errors in a single digit; both of those were in the standby position, but one was the MVN ATIS frequency. Since the in-use frequency on that transceiver was that of MVN tower, and a pilot would usually listen to the ATIS before switching to tower frequency, one could speculate that Kennedy had not heard the ATIS. Still 20 miles out, Kennedy had yet not contacted the tower.

The VHF nav in-use and standby frequencies were set for four VORs along the route; none was tuned to the MVY VOR, however, nor was the ADF tuned to the nearby Edgartown beacon. The implication of the settings is that Kennedy must have been using the GPS for primary guidance.

The "obvious" explanation of the accident, to which every armchair analyst gravitated within hours of the first news broadcasts, was spatial disorientation and/or vertigo. Several pages of the final report are devoted to a general exposition of the subject of spatial disorientation. There is a hint that it could have been brought on by the stooping motion needed to reach the fuel valve; selecting the fuller tank would have been a natural pre-approach action. In keeping with a general principle of accident investigation that uncommon events should be traced, if possible, to commonplace causes, the NTSB does not venture into alternative theories. For instance, Kennedy might have been using the autopilot; under the circumstances, in fact, most pilots would have. It could have suffered some sort of failure and begun making uncommanded turns, and Kennedy might have recognized the problem and switched the autopilot off, but too late to recover. There is no evidence for such a scenario, but there is equally little evidence for spatial disorientation, other than the fact of the accident itself.

The NTSB's report on the Kennedy accident is, in fact, an extremely detailed analysis without any definite or illuminating conclusion. The "probable cause" was just as probable before the investigation and analysis as after it. Accidents attributable to spatial disorientation or to various kinds of visual illusions are fairly common over water and unlighted terrain, and are routinely disposed of with brief and perfunctory reports. Because of Kennedy's celebrity, his accident — an accident like all accidents — merited more. It became one of those events "that alter and illuminate our times."

My Boat So Small

In March, 2012 in southern Georgia, a hot-air balloon
was sucked into a thunderstorm. Carried to 17,000 feet in
an updraft, battered by one-inch hail, its fabric envelope
split open and collapsed. Only four days later did
searchers finally locate it in a forested area miles from
the launch point. Large clumps of compacted hail were
still enfolded among the ruins of the envelope. Though
the open wicker gondola was practically undamaged, the
pilot in it was dead.

According to a local news report at the time, no autopsy
was to be performed, but a CT scan of the body revealed
a broken spine, which was said to be the cause of death.
No medical information, or comment on survivability, is
provided in the National Transportation Safety Board's
report of the accident.

News media, as well as the balloonist's many friends and admirers, adopted a heroic scenario in which the balloonist, who was carrying seven skydivers, climbed to an altitude from which he was certain they could jump safely, then told them to jump, sacrificing himself to save them.

The NTSB took a somewhat more dry-eyed view of the accident. The cause, it declared, was "the pilot's intentional flight into adverse weather. Contributing to the accident was the pilot's failure to obtain a weather briefing and his failure to follow the balloon manufacturer's published emergency procedure for weather deterioration during flight."The manufacturer's emergency procedure alluded to is colorfully phrased: "land immediately rather than fly into severe atmospheric turmoil."

Neither view, in my opinion, captures the nuances of this accident.

The "hero saves parachutists, sacrifices self" version doesn't make much sense. The standard minimum altitude for deploying a sport parachute is 2,000 feet. The first group of three jumpers left the gondola at above 5,000 feet, the rest above 6,000. The jumpers were never in danger. Clearly, if it had been purely a matter of ensuring everyone's safety, the pilot could have sent them out much earlier, or could simply have aborted the mission when it became apparent that a thunderstorm

26

was building nearby and the balloon was heading toward it.

The NTSB's finding that the pilot failed to obtain a weather briefing is probably misleading. To begin with, hot-air balloons are flown only in a very limited range of conditions, light surface winds being a basic requirement for getting inflated and airborne in the first place. Furthermore, a balloon flight with skydivers is not like a cross-country flight in an airplane. The balloonist is concerned, unlike the cross-country pilot, with weather in his immediate vicinity — in other words, with what he can see with his own eyes. Furthermore, the fact that the pilot had not spoken to a flight service station briefer or contacted a DUATS site does not mean that he did not study the weather. There are many sources of weather information that do not record the identity of those who consult them, and the pilot had already made several previous flights that day and was quite aware of the local conditions.

The information that the NTSB apparently supposes that the pilot overlooked or ignored was a convective SIGMET covering a long, narrow quadrilateral with the launch site in the acute angle of its extreme southwest corner. But there is no reason to suppose that he was unaware of it. A SIGMET is not a prediction of particular conditions at a particular place; it merely warns of possible conditions over a large region. One frequently flies through SIGMET areas, circumnavigating isolated storms.

x Significent Meteorological information

As practitioners of extreme sports often do, the seven skydivers had brought along their video cameras, and the entire final flight, until the departure of the last jumper, was covered with a thoroughness that would have done credit to Cecil B. DeMille. Some of the tape footage, edited into a tribute to the late pilot, may be found on YouTube (www.youtube.com/watch? v=Vd5VLWIxBAE). Between the YouTube video and the ground crew chief's running conversation with the pilot, little about the flight is left to the imagination.

The storm that would swallow the balloon is glimpsed at the start of the video as a gleaming tower of white cumulus against the background of a benign blue sky. In the jolly chaos of launching in a freshening breeze, its portentous presence is seemingly ignored. The red, white and black balloon, 67 feet high and levitated by 105,000 cubic feet of heated air, then rises obliquely toward the cloud.

Between the drift of the balloon and the expansion of the storm, by the time the balloon had reached 5,380 feet it was floating close beneath a shelf of gray cloud. The pilot was aware of the nearby storm; a warning had been relayed to him by the ground crew. Besides, it looked somewhat menacing: In the video, one helmet camera repeatedly swings aside to settle for a moment upon the gray columns of rain and shadow beneath it. Though the altitude is lower than originally planned, a cameraman pushes off on his back, facing the gondola, followed by two jumpers. A moment later the pilot is heard asking his ground crew whether the storm is building or dissipating; they tell him it is growing rapidly.

The balloon continues to ascend. Two more jumpers go out at 6,380 feet, now in cloud. On footage recorded by the camera of one of the last two jumpers, the pilot is seen gesturing impatiently; he seems to be telling them to go without further delay. That is the last we see of the pilot and the gondola.

All of the jumpers reach the landing zone safely. One says to another, "It was choppy up there, huh?" "Yeah," the other replies. "That was *sick*. In a storm."

"Sick" means "great" when you've gotten tired of saying "awesome."

According to the crew chief, while the balloon was still visible from the ground the pilot radioed that he would try to climb above the storm, whose size and power he clearly underestimated; its towering core was hidden from his view. After the balloon disappeared into the cloud base, the ground crew, one of whose jobs is to rejoin the balloon wherever it lands, headed in the general direction that the storm was moving while receiving continuous updates from the pilot.

Attempting to top the storm, the pilot reported from 8,000 feet that the winds were strong and swirling and "this [is] not going to be good." At 12,000 feet he had given up hope of climbing over. He was in heavy hail and rising rapidly in an updraft. "He went from 15,000 to 17,000 much quicker," the crew chief later reported, "than he had been calling out 1,000 foot increments."

The Firefly 8 balloon was equipped with a "parachute valve," a large disk of fabric at the top of the envelope whose perimeter can be pulled inward, allowing hot air to escape for a rapid descent; but it was in updrafts so strong that the parachute valve would have been ineffective in any case.

Then the pilot's voice altered. The balloon had collapsed and was falling now, and again and again, as he called out his altitude, he said, "I've got nothing over my head." He did not release the transmit key. The crew chief listened helplessly to the litany of diminishing altitudes until at last the pilot said, "I am at 2,000 feet I see trees I'm in the trees I am at 1,000 feet I'm not gonna make it I'm sorry."

Desperately pursuing the balloon through torrents of rain and hail, the chase car crashed into a ditch. Four inches of hailstones the size of walnuts accumulated on the ground in two minutes. In the half-hour bracketing the accident, meteorological recording equipment tallied over 1,000 lighting strikes beneath the storm, which rapidly reached Level 5 or 6 intensity — severe to extreme — with tops at 37,000 feet. It then dissipated as quickly as it had formed.

There is nothing in the video the suggest that the jumpers had any inkling that their flight would put the pilot at risk. The pilot, evidently reluctant to disappoint his excited passengers, kept the knowledge of the danger to himself. The risk was all his. He did not deliberately sacrifice himself to save them; he optimistically and generously miscalculated the risk he was running in providing them with the jumps they had anticipated.

The image of a single man tossed about in an open wicker basket at 17,000 feet in a thunderstorm is hard to get out of one's mind. It is the quintessence of tragic solitude, like a sailor lost overboard in a raging sea or a space explorer marooned on a receding asteroid. No longer merely a man, he is a metaphor for our worst fears of defeat and abandonment. There is an epic grandeur in that, but still — poor guy!

A Substantial Amount for Dinner

FAA regulations are highly specific, and suspected violations may at times be subjected to extremely literal-minded scrutiny. On the other hand, an FAA publication entitled "Aeronautical Decision Making" takes a somewhat more practical view of the realities of day-to-day flying, and concedes, according to a National Transportation Safety Board paraphrase, that "pilots, particularly those with considerable experience, try to complete flights as planned, please passengers, and meet schedules, which can compromise safety and impose an unrealistic assessment of piloting skill under stressful conditions." In other words, pilots — especially experienced ones — take chances. But why should highly *experienced* pilots be particularly prone to risk-taking? The reason, I suspect, is that they've been there before, seen it all, and been successful taking similar risks in the past. They believe in themselves. After all, risk is not a certainty, but merely an increased probability, of misfortune. One may elude many dangers, becoming accustomed to them, until (perhaps) the odds finally catch up.

In March, 2001, a chartered Gulfstream III carrying two pilots, a flight attendant, and 15 passengers crashed a quarter-mile short of the runway at Aspen, Colorado. All aboard the plane died. The accident took place at about 7:00 p.m. Official night, which begins 30 minutes after sunset, had only just begun; but in fact it was quite dark, the sun having disappeared below the surrounding mountaintops 79 minutes earlier. Although the airport's automated weather observation system was reporting calm wind and good visibility, scattered light snow showers were falling, the ceiling was broken and variable, and one witness described conditions at the airport around the time of the accident as "socking in" with fog and decreasing visibility.

The flight, which originated at Los Angeles International Airport, had been scheduled to depart at 3:30 PST, but passengers arrived late and the Gulfstream was not airborne until 4:11. The pilots were aware that their late departure posed a problem: noise restrictions prevented the GIII from landing at Aspen once legal night had begun. According to their flight plan, they would arrive with only 12 minutes to spare.

The Aspen airport lies in a narrow valley surrounded on three sides by very steep and high terrain. The nominal runway elevation is 7,815 ft, but the runway slopes, and the threshold of Runway 15 is at 7,674 ft. The initial fix for the VOR-DME stepdown approach is the Red Table VOR, located 12.4 miles from the runway threshold on a bearing of 344 degrees. The MDA for class A through C aircraft (that is, those having approach speeds, defined as 1.3 times the stalling speed, gear and flaps down, at maximum landing weight, of up to 140 knots) is 10,200 ft, 2,526 above the runway threshold. Approaches are not authorized for Class D aircraft, whose approach speed is greater than 140 knots. The GIII, with an approach speed of 138 knots, qualifies as a Class C aircraft.

The Missed Approach Point (MAP) is 1.4 nm from the threshold; thus, a pilot who is at the MAP when he catches sight of the runway would have to descend almost 2,500 feet in that distance. Even at an approach speed of 90 knots, a descent rate of more than 2,500 feet per minute would be required. The approach is therefore classed as a circling approach, even though the 16-degree misalignment of the runway with respect to the approach course falls within the definition of "straight-in." The fact that an approach is classified as circling, however, does not preclude pilots' landing straight in if conditions allow a "normal" approach.

The missed approach procedure makes use of a supplementary localizer back course, offset from the

runway, to keep climbing aircraft away from the
mountains south of the airport.

When this unusual instrument approach was first
instituted in 1988, night approaches were not allowed,
but in 1994 the FAA bowed to pressure from users of the
airport and removed the night restriction. Seven years
later, in March, 2001, an FAA flight inspection team
noted that "areas of unlighted terrain conflicted with
traffic patterns and circling descent maneuvers near the
airport," and concluded that circling should not be
allowed at night. A permanent NOTAM was promptly
published that eliminated all circling minimums at night.
The wording of the NOTAM was murky, however; it left
unclear whether what had been eliminated was *any* night
use of the approach, or only the authorization to circle.
The FAA's interpretation, and the only logical one, was
that since no straight-in minimums existed the NOTAM
implicitly eliminated night use of the approach
altogether. That the NOTAM didn't simply say this was
due to the loss of capacity for honest, direct and clear
communication that is endemic in the government. After
the GIII accident, someone who could write plain
English was located and a revised, unambiguous
NOTAM was published.

The NOTAM was widely disseminated, but strangely
enough one place that didn't get it was the control tower
at Aspen. If the local controller there had known about
the NOTAM — and had been able to decipher its intent
— she would have been required to inform arriving pilots

that night approaches were no longer authorized. The crew of the GIII had received the NOTAM from the Hawthorne FSS in Los Angeles, but may not have considered it of decisive importance for two reasons. First, it appeared to refer only to circling maneuvers; and second, they expected to arrive a few minutes before legal night.

As the GIII was embarking passengers, one of the pilots remarked that they might have to divert to nearby Rifle. When the charter customer, whose guests the passengers were and who was on the flight himself, heard of this he became "irate" and instructed his assistant to call the charter operator and tell them that "the airplane was not going to be redirected." He had flown into ASE at night before, he said, and was going to do it again. The assistant (who was not on the flight) transmitted the decree as directed. Another pilot who worked for the company later told investigators, however, that management "would have placed no pressure on the captain to land at ASE." Still, the captain was aware of the demand of his imperious passenger, because at one point during the flight he said via radio to a company scheduler that it was important for them to land at Aspen because "the customer [had] spent a substantial amount of money on dinner."

In violation of company policy, the captain allowed one of the passengers to sit in the cockpit jumpseat during the approach. Whether this was the customer or one of his guests is unknown, although his voice can be heard on the CVR tape. If it was the customer, the pressure on the crew to complete the approach was no doubt increased.

Although it was certainly darker than they would have liked, the ATIS provided the crew with a promising picture of the weather: 10 miles visibility, 2,000 scattered, 5,500 broken. This report was an hour old; but it may have suggested that by descending below 2,000 feet agl — several hundred feet below the MDA — the crew would be able to get a look at the runway.

The captain was the pilot flying. Two other jets missed approaches ahead of them, but the GIII's pilots seem to have entered into a tacit agreement to try to get into Aspen come what may. A shared feeling that what they were about to do could involve some improvisation might explain the captain's failure to perform the approach briefing as required and the first officer's failure to make many of the required altitude callouts or to offer any comment when, after reaching the MDA, the captain continued to descend even though neither pilot had the airport or the approach lights in sight. The airplane's dual automated altitude alerting systems dutifully called out heights above the ground as the GIII dropped steadily lower and lower and the two pilots, glimpsing miscellaneous roads, towns and rivers through the intermittent snow, tried in vain to find the runway lights.

Automatic altitude alerts crowded the final seconds of the flight. Just after a sink rate alert from the ground proximity warning system and a 400-foot altitude callout from the flight profile advisory unit, the captain brought the engines up to maximum power. At this point, however, the terrain was rising under the airplane, and 300- and 200-foot warnings followed in rapid succession. Perhaps realizing at the last moment that the airplane was to the right of the runway centerline and extremely close to the ground, the captain rolled it into a 40-degree left bank. When the GIII's left wing struck the ground, the pilot's altimeter would have been showing an altitude *below* the published field elevation.

The NTSB found that the probable cause of the accident was "the flight crew's operation of the airplane below minimum descent altitude without an appropriate visual reference for the runway." Among contributing factors it cited the ambiguous wording of the FAA's NOTAM and the failure of the NOTAM even to reach the Aspen tower; the inability of the crew to see the terrain because of darkness, mist and snow; and pressure on the captain to land from both the charter customer and the noise-related night landing restriction.

This accident attracted some publicity because of its lifestyles-of-the-rich-and-famous aspect. Pilots discussed it and study groups used it as a case in point. How in the world did two experienced pilots — they had 15,000 hours between them — persuade themselves to deviate so far from what was permissible and proper as to find themselves *below* the still-unseen runway on short final? Was this a case of some sort of mutual temporary insanity? Was it a completely-off-the-chart freak event? Or was this the kind of thing that some flight crews would do quite regularly? After all, many an airplane has struck terrain during an instrument approach, and this can happen only if the pilot ignores the parameters of the approach. This was not, in short, an isolated event. It was symptomatic of an underlying flaw in a system that relies for its effectiveness on unswervingly mechanical execution of simple rules. The flaw is that those rules are being executed by human beings.

Obviously, this accident would not have occurred if the captain had leveled out at the MDA. He would not have seen the runway, and he would have missed the approach and proceeded to the alternate. Presumably the other airplanes that approached before him and missed did just that. But instead he paused only briefly at the MDA before continuing his descent at a steady rate that was, in fact, quite accurately calculated to bring him to the runway threshold — if only he could have found it.

The moment he left the MDA he was in violation, because, as far as it's possible to tell from the CVR tape, neither pilot ever saw the runway. They did at one point tell the local controller that they had the runway in sight, but all indications are that in fact they did not. They could see other bits and pieces of landscape, however, which may have supported the belief that once they got below the cloud deck they would be in the clear. Nevertheless, it was the duty of the first officer to warn the pilot that he was descending below the MDA. Why did he remain silent? In part, perhaps, because the action was so obviously deliberate that to mention it would have been to challenge the captain's authority and, in effect, to accuse him of a violation. Nevertheless, the first officer might still have done it if there had not been a third party in the cockpit. The presence of an outsider, particular if it were the headstrong customer who paid for the trip, or even someone perceived as his representative, might inhibit confrontational-seeming behavior by a junior crew member.

The crux of the accident was the obvious failure of the crew to act as two independent equals rather than as an omnipotent superior and a silent subordinate. Under the circumstances — as is quite clear in retrospect — the captain should have flown the approach exactly by the book, and, if it failed, gone to the alternate. He should have told the angry customer to take his complaints, and, if need be, his business, elsewhere. *Should have*; yet any introspective pilot who has experienced a similar situation can understand its psychology: the implicit challenge to the captain's abilities and nerve, the need to rise to the occasion rather than appear to take the easy way out, even the tempting glory of successfully plucking forbidden fruit. There is only one way to be perfectly safe in situations like this: it is to be mechanical rather than human.

Vectors to ZMB

A C35 Bonanza, N5946C, was cruising at 6,500 feet when there was a sudden loud sound from the engine compartment, followed by a smell of oil. The engine sputtered and lost power.

The 3,300-hour commercial pilot, 59, who was taking his single passenger on an air taxi flight from central Long Island to a destination in New Jersey, initially, and appropriately, reacted by pulling up to slow the airplane and gain a couple of hundred feet of altitude.

The engine failure took place at approximately 0738:40 local time, a few seconds after the JFK departure controller who had cleared 46C into JFK Class B handed the flight off to LaGuardia departure. At that moment, the Bonanza's heading was 282 degrees and it was

making a 142-knot groundspeed against a headwind of
20 to 25 knots.

About 80 seconds after the engine failure, at 0739:58, the
controller gave 46C a right turn to 360. At that point the
Bonanza had lost 1,000 feet in altitude and its
groundspeed had slowed to 62 knots, circumstances that,
oddly, did not elicit any comment from the controller.
Only now did the pilot explain his situation: "Okay, 46C,
I'm having a little bit of a problem, it's, ah, I may have to
turn to Farmingdale, well, give me a second if I may..."

The controller twice urged the pilot to "keep me in the
loop [and] let me know what's going on [and] any
assistance you need." At 0740:31, the pilot, without
declaring an emergency, said, "I'm gonna have to take it
down at the closest spot."

The controller immediately reeled off a list of
possibilities: LaGuardia, Kennedy, Westchester,
Republic Airport at Farmingdale (FRG).

"Okay," the pilot replied, "Farmingdale is the closest
airport, nine miles, okay, yeah, I'm not going to make
Farmingdale." As he said this, the pilot began a left turn
toward FRG, then about 140 degrees from his position.
He was now at 3,500 feet.

His estimate that he could not make FRG was correct.
According to the C35 POH, the airplane would glide 1.7
nm per 1,000 feet of altitude — a glide ratio of 10 to one

— at its best glide speed of 105 kias and with the windmilling prop at the minimum rpm setting. We do not know what, if anything, the pilot did about the prop pitch, but his speed, which varied between 80 and 90 knots over the ground even after he had turned southeastward and put the wind a little behind him, was too low for optimum performance. At any rate, he could no longer expect to glide more than six nautical miles.

Then came a lifeline. "There is a strip about your 10 o'clock and five miles," the controller said. "Bethpage Airport." The pilot grasped at it. "Give me this airport," he said, "I'm not seeing it."

"There's a strip right about at your 12 o'clock and three miles ... the strip is a closed airport, ah, I just know there is a runway there, about 11 o'clock and about a mile and a half now."

The Bonanza was at 1,400 feet msl. The pilot searched for the runway, but saw only buildings.

The controller continued to vector the pilot while offering alternatives: a parkway right below him, FRG's big runway still five miles distant.

"Yeah, no way on that, let's see, uh, tell me this strip again if you would, I'm sorry."

"There's a strip about one o'clock and less than a mile," the controller repeated, "it's a closed airport, I have no information about it unfortunately."

The pilot never found the Bethpage runway. He tried to land on railroad tracks, but luck was not with him. His right wing struck a barrier at the only grade crossing in the vicinity, and the airplane flipped over and broke into flame. The pilot died of impact trauma and burns; the passenger survived with serious injuries.

The reason the pilot had failed to find the Bethpage Airport — formerly the home of the Grumman Aircraft Corporation — was that it did not exist, having been replaced several years earlier by an industrial park.

The reason the controller vectored him to it was that the nonexistent Bethpage runway was still depicted on his radar screen.

It emerged from the National Transportation Safety Board's investigation of this accident that the FAA lacked a formal procedure for ensuring that closed airports were purged from the radar video maps used by controllers. Nonetheless, someone had removed the Bethpage runway from the radar video maps of JFK and Islip controllers, whose coverage overlapped LaGuardia's. The zombie airport remained only on LaGuardia controllers' screens.

The NTSB identified other contributing factors. Of course, there was the engine failure; the crankshaft had broken, there was a hole in the oil sump, and the engine was incapable of producing power. In addition, there was the cocktail of drugs, including amphetamine at more than 12 times therapeutic levels, that post mortem toxicology found in the pilot's blood and urine. The combination of the drugs he was taking or abusing and the medical conditions for which they had been prescribed "likely significantly impaired his psychomotor functioning and decision-making."

What primarily caused the accident, the NTSB found, was not so much a decision as the lack of one.

When the engine failed, the Bonanza was about seven nm from the FRG runway and could have glided more than 10 nm, assuming that the POH numbers are correct and that the pilot had executed the glide in accordance with POH instructions. Naturally, there was bound to be some delay while the pilot assessed the situation and, according to the surviving passenger, tried to restart the engine. This took time. Nevertheless, two minutes and 15 seconds elapsed between the engine failure and the pilot's finally starting a turn toward FRG.

The pilot had been operating an on-demand charter service out of Westhampton, where the flight originated, for a dozen years, and it's certain that he was quite familiar with FRG and knew that it was a few miles behind him and to the left when the engine quit. Yet, all the while he was losing precious altitude he did not take the precaution of turning toward it. Nor did he explain his 1,000-fpm descent to the controller, nor report that he had engine trouble, nor ask — though he almost certainly already knew the answer — for a vector to the closest runway.

Few pilots ever experience a total engine failure. When one does, it is nearly always his first. Impeccable reactions cannot be expected. Nevertheless, like the prospect of being hanged in a fortnight, sudden silence "concentrates his mind wonderfully." The pilot's first action — to pull up to convert speed to altitude — was correct. His second should have been to turn toward FRG — but he did not do so until he had gone so far, and lost so much altitude, that FRG was no longer within his reach.

The pilot might still have salvaged the situation by landing on any of several golf courses, or on the parkway that the controller pointed out to him, if only he had not been led to believe — because of a grotesque and cruel bureaucratic oversight — that a runway lay just ahead.

Pilots reading this account will be relieved to know that the FAA now has a formal procedure for purging nonexistent airports from controllers' data bases. You have to wonder, though: Why didn't they think of that before?

Funny Stuff

In November, 2007, a flight school's Piper Arrow disintegrated during a cross-country training flight, killing a flight instructor and his student. Another student pilot, an Italian, who was riding along in the back seat to increase his familiarity with English-language radio jargon, also perished in the crash. The airplane came to earth in a number of pieces, widely scattered. The outer panels of both wings had separated, the right wing failing upward and forward, the left downward, leaving the inboard eight or ten feet attached to the fuselage. The forward fuselage, including the windshield frame, instrument panel and control yokes had separated from the cabin, as had the tail cone and empennage, and the roof of the cabin itself had been ripped off, leaving the occupants to descend from 10,000 feet in an open tub with useless stumps for wings.

The flight instructor had approximately 600 hours, 300 of which he had logged in the previous three months. Apparently a prodigy of sorts, he had earned his private license in 56 hours in 2004 but had then ceased flying. Resuming after a hiatus of three years, in less than five months he became a single- and multi-engine and instrument instructor. A few days after getting his CFII he completed "new flight instructor training" at the flight school. Everyone agreed that he was an excellent pilot; one of his fellow instructors called him "the best pilot he'd ever flown with."

After the accident, the National Transportation Safety Board investigator in charge received a copy of an email that the Italian student had sent to some friends a week before the crash. The investigator had two translations made; the following is my paraphrase of them:

"Yesterday I went up as a passenger with a megalomaniac instructor to listen to radio communications, which are incredible. Unfortunately, there are two air traffic controllers, one of whom sounds like he's dying when he talks, and the other one talks in code...

"But I was telling you about the megalomaniac instructor. Yesterday we were flying along and he suddenly took the controls and without any warning he did a two-turn spin [or two rolls]. I was practically thrown overboard — my seat belt was loose because we weren't supposed to do any aerobatics. But it was a lot of fun."

A megalomaniac is a person who is obsessed with the idea of his own importance or greatness. Often such an obsession is unconnected with reality and becomes a "delusion of grandeur," but it is also possible for a person to be genuinely important or great and still be a megalomaniac. In any case, psychological terminology is used very imprecisely in casual conversation, and it is impossible to know exactly what the student meant when he applied the term to the instructor. Besides, as the NTSB report on the accident cautiously notes, it could not be *definitively* established that the instructor the Italian student referred to as a "megalomaniac" was the one involved in the accident.

Nevertheless, interviews with other instructors at the school revealed that the instructor involved in the accident was known to perform spins, barrel rolls and "snap rolls" with students in airplanes not approved for aerobatics. Some utility-category airplanes are approved for spins, which are a relatively low-stress maneuver that is not considered aerobatic; spin approval has more to do with the recovery behavior of different aircraft types than with structural issues. Rolls are a different story. Although a barrel roll, properly executed, involves even lower stresses than a spin recovery does, barrel rolls are aerobatic maneuvers (formally defined as ones involving more than 60 degrees of bank or 30 degrees of pitch) and are not permitted in any normal- or utility-category airplane. The FARs require that parachutes be worn whenever aerobatic maneuvers are performed and that aerobatic airplanes have means of emergency egress, such as jettisonable doors.

One instructor — the Italian was her student, and she had suggested that he go on the accident flight to increase his familiarity with radio communications — told investigators that she knew that the accident instructor sometimes demonstrated spins to his students. She considered this unnecessary, since knowledge of spin recovery was not required at this stage of their training, but evidently she did not think it harmful. She did report, however, that although she "felt completely safe with his flying abilities" she had asked him, during lunch on the very day of the accident, to refrain from "funny stuff" while her student was along. She did not want him to contract any "bad habits."

Another instructor, the one who called the accident instructor "the best pilot he had ever flown with," reported that the latter had once told him he had performed a "snap roll" in one of the training planes, and that he had "expressed his displeasure" at hearing it. The investigator asked him to describe how a "snap roll" is executed. He replied that "the airplane is nosed over until 140 knots is reached. The pilot then pitches up until about 10 to 15 degrees above the horizon. The pilot then applies left rudder and aileron."

50

Another student described a "barrel roll" performed by
the accident instructor in similar terms — 140-knot entry
speed, pitch up, etc — and noted that it was a smooth
maneuver, not a violent one. This is, in fact, the
description of a barrel roll, not a snap roll, which is a sort
of horizontal spin classically entered at low to moderate
speed with a sudden simultaneous application of full
rudder and up elevator, not aileron. A snap roll is, as the
name suggests, a comparatively violent maneuver,
although it may not put excessive stress on the airframe
if it is performed at a sufficiently low speed.

Radar records of the Arrow's final flight showed a series
of five "maneuvers of interest," all conducted at high
altitude — above 10,000 feet — and involving a dive to
gain speed followed by a climb and, in the first four
cases, an eventual level-out at 90 knots. In the first four
maneuvers, the speed did not exceed 120 kcas — that is,
120 knots indicated airspeed, corrected for instrument
error. In the final maneuver the airplane accelerated to
134 kcas before beginning to decelerate and then
disappearing from radar.

 The radar records of these "maneuvers of interest" give
no information about the attitude of the airplane, but the
first four could be consistent with a series of barrel rolls.
The structural failures that apparently occurred during
the fifth maneuver, however, are more suggestive of
something akin to a snap roll, or at any rate of an abrupt
rolling pull-up executed at high speed.

The probable cause of the accident, the NTSB said, was "the pilot's intentional performance of aerobatic maneuvers that exceeded the design limits of the airplane structure." Although the NTSB investigator examined the pilot's logbook, the accident report makes no mention of the pilot ever having received aerobatic instruction. The report also does not reveal whether the operators of the flight school were aware of the instructor's propensity for impromptu aerobatics, and if so what they thought of it.

The Arrow is a normal category airplane, not approved for spins or for any type of aerobatics. Its limit positive load factor is 3.8 G's, and its maneuvering speed is 116 kcas. The pilot seems to have begun his final maneuver, whatever it was, above that speed, but, as my readers know, since I let hardly a month go by without mentioning it, even being at or below maneuvering speed does not give pilots carte blanche. Maneuvering speed is predicated on the wing stalling before the limit load factor is exceeded in a positive-G wings-level pull-up; it does not guarantee that the airframe can survive every other maneuver or combination of control deflections. In this case, the structural failure seem to have been the result of a combination of wing torsion and bending, caused by a sudden and simultaneous deflection of at least the elevator and ailerons, and perhaps of the rudder as well . The instructor may have overcontrolled because of the presence of a passenger in the back seat; as the CG moves aft, pitch control forces diminish.

There exists among pilots a double standard with respect to the relationship between skill and what may, for lack of a more precise term, be called "goodness." An analogy may be made with drivers. Many who are highly skilled are also overconfident, ostentatious and incautious; and so they are not "good drivers" in an insurance company's sense of the term. With pilots, similarly, one can differentiate between those whose goodness consists of the ability to execute complex maneuvers precisely and those whose goodness consists in the ability — certainly more important from a passenger's standpoint — to bring everybody back to earth safe and sound and with dry sick-sacks. But cautious, responsible and conservative flying impresses no one.

We don't know exactly what the unfortunate Italian student meant by the word "megalomaniac," but probably he intended to suggest a certain boldness, ostentation, and grandiosity in the flying style of the instructor. Such an attitude, which is consistent with a known propensity for startling passengers with unannounced rolls and spins, may win the respect of young students intoxicated with romantic ideas about flight. But the desire to impress is a trait that pilots ought to distrust in others and in themselves. Unchecked, it can produce disastrous results.

Sunday Drive

At about 8:25 a.m. on the morning of September 3, 2007, Steve Fossett took off from a friend's ranch, about 60 miles southeast of Reno, in a borrowed 1980 Bellanca Super Decathlon. A few minutes later, about nine miles south of the airstrip, an employee of the ranch, who knew the airplane well, saw the Decathlon fly past 150 or 200 feet above the ground.

Fossett did not come back. The search for him, unusually intense because of Fossett's prominence, wealth, and wide connections in aeronautical circles, turned up nothing, and in due course it was suspended. Although his buddy Richard Branson predicted that he might, Fossett did not hike out of the wilderness unharmed. He was declared legally dead after five months, and fanciful theories began to sprout that he had faked his death in

order to escape money troubles or to settle, heavily
bearded, in the South Seas with a beautiful mistress.

Thirteen months after Fossett's disappearance, a Sierra
hiker chanced upon some papers that were his. Searchers
returned to the area, and two days later the severely
fragmented wreckage of the Decathlon was located about
half a mile from the first find. Fire had consumed most of
what might have been visible to aerial searchers, who
had flown over the debris without noticing it.

There was nothing in the wreckage to suggest a
mechanical problem. Both propeller blades, which had
broken out of the hub, showed the type of bending and
scoring that indicates that the engine was developing
power at impact. The aluminum wing structure — the
airplane, originally equipped with a fabric-covered wood
wing, had been re-winged in 1996 — was severely
twisted and mangled, but the strut attachments were
secure. The engine, found a hundred feet uphill from the
main wreckage, was heavily damaged. Investigators
concluded that the airplane had been in level flight and a
right bank, moving at a relatively high speed, when it
struck the southern flank of a northwest-southeast
oriented ridge at about the 10,000-foot level.

A 20-minute radar track that began at 9:07 a.m. and led
almost directly to the accident site had earlier been
ignored by accident investigators because the ranch
employee who had seen Fossett fly past had put the
sighting at around 9:30, based on a cell phone

conversation he had at the time. A belated check of telephone company records revealed that the call had actually taken place at 8:30, and the seemingly inconsistent radar track then seemed likely to be that of the Decathlon. It began about 35 miles south-southwest of the ranch with several minutes of beacon returns squawking 1200 and reporting Mode C altitudes of 14,500 to 14,900 feet. The transponder returns then ceased, and the remainder of the track consisted of primary echoes ending about a mile northwest of the accident site.

Arguing for the identification of the radar track as Fossett's was not only its termination close to the accident site, but the fact that its starting point, at 14,500 feet — 1,500 feet above the mountaintops — was not inconsistent with the witness sighting half an hour earlier. The Super Decathlon, climbing on the lee side of the mountains — the wind was out of the south-southwest at an estimated 18 knots, gusting to 34 — would have required less than half an hour for the 9,000-foot altitude gain, and it was not unlikely that it might have traveled 26 nm while climbing against the wind. In level flight and descending, during the 20-minute duration of the radar track, it averaged only 90 knots. The NTSB did not comment upon the sudden appearance of the track — which may have been due to incomplete radar coverage — or upon the termination, after several minutes, of the transponder returns.

A camper reported having seen what he believed was Fossett's airplane flying southward. He said that it "looked like it was standing still due to the wind." The camper's sighting, at "a little before 1000" and 30 miles from the accident site, did not mesh well with the NTSB's timeline, but the observation was one of several that the NTSB included to bolster its finding that the probable cause of the crash was "downdrafts that exceeded the climb capability of the airplane." Other pilots who had flown in the area that day gave mixed reports. One said it was "a wonderful day to go flying," with 10-knot winds aloft and no "big turbulence." Another characterized the day as "weird," "unusually smooth [with] random rough chop."

Based on the forecast winds aloft, the NTSB decided that "moderate turbulence ... probably occurred." A computer simulation predicted downdrafts of as much as 400 feet per minute — that is, about four knots. The airplane's manual claimed a climb rate of 300 fpm at the prevailing density altitude of 13,000 feet.

Returning to comb the area nearly a month after the discovery of the wreckage, sheriffs found clothing, credit cards, Fossett's driver's license, and a few bones that were subsequently determined by DNA testing to be his. The cause of death, based on these "skeletal fragments," was determined, in a bold forensic leap, to be "multiple traumatic injuries." Nevertheless, the distance between the wreckage and the remains, and the fact that both front-seat belt buckles (the airplane had both five-point acrobatic and standard seat belts for both seats) were found unlatched, suggested to some that Fossett might have survived the crash and moved several hundred yards before succumbing to his injuries.

The fanciful speculation that Fossett had faked his own death dwindled once the airplane, the personal effects and the bones had been found. The real mystery was a less titillating one: How, or why, did a 6,000-hour ATP fly into a mountain in broad daylight?

Unfortunately, the only evidence of anything resembling pilot intention is the disappearance of the transponder signal, at an altitude of 14,900 feet. Three interpretations are possible: The transponder could have failed spontaneously, the receiving station could have failed for some reason to pick up its returns, or Fossett himself could have turned it off. Since the area is very close to Yosemite National Park, and low flight within national parks is frowned upon, it is conceivable that Fossett, having decided to get down closer to the terrain and being uncertain of his exact relation to the park, turned off the transponder in an exercise, so to speak, of his fifth amendment rights.

Clearly, Fossett must have been flying low in order to hit the mountain; a 400-fpm downdraft could not possibly produce a loss of thousands of feet of altitude followed by an uncontrolled collision with a ridge. There were too many escape routes. But the downdraft theory may appear inconsistent with a high-speed impact. A

Decathlon caught in a downdraft and struggling to avoid terrain would most likely be flying slowly, not fast.

But slow is relative. Fossett, who owned and flew a Citation X, may have been reluctant to get the Decathlon as slow as it could really go, especially while turning hard in turbulence. At that density altitude 70 kias is 85 ktas, and if he had a 20-knot wind behind him he could actually have been moving at 105 knots — perhaps fast enough to account for the condition of the wreckage. A problem with the downdraft-plus-wind scenario, however, is that Fossett crashed into a windward slope; there should have been an updraft, not a downdraft.

Another possibility, which the NTSB does not mention, is what might be called the Cory Lidle scenario. Lidle was the Yankees pitcher who crashed his plane into a Manhattan apartment building in 2006 while trying to reverse course within the confines of the East River. A strong east wind was blowing. If Lidle and his instructor had been flying along the downwind edge of the river and turned into the wind, they would have completed the turn safely; but they were flying along the upwind edge, and the wind carried them over into Manhattan.

Fossett crashed on the northeastern slope of a valley that ascended toward the northwest. It is possible that, flying generally northwestward, he had descended deeper into the valley than he intended — perhaps because of a downdraft from the southwestern slope — and then tried to escape by making a right turn. The wind, blowing

from the southwest, possibly gusty, and gaining speed
near the ridge, could have carried him wide, into the
mountain.

It has been seen as ironic that Fossett, who had made so
many remarkable flights, including three solo nonstop
trips around the world in the GlobalFlyer and the first
solo balloon circumnavigation of the globe, and had
collected so many world records, should end his life on a
mere Sunday drive. It was as if a soldier, after surviving
many battles, should succumb to an infected bug bite.
But Fossett did not accomplish his feats by being overly
fussy about danger or averse to thrills. The risk in
swooping down for a closer look at the Sierra landscape
may have seemed acceptable, even beneath his notice. In
aviation, there is no paradox in being cut down by a
small danger after having eluded big ones; the one that
gets you is big enough.

John Denver

The singer John Denver was an experienced pilot. When he applied to renew his medical certificate in June, 1996, he reported a total flight time of 2,750 hours. He held a private certificate with instrument, multi, seaplane and glider ratings, as well as a Learjet type rating. He had experience in a wide variety of aircraft types. And so when he died in a crash in the course of a routine VFR sightseeing flight on October 12, 1997, speculation about the cause of the accident — of which there was a great deal, as always happens when a celebrity dies in a plane crash — centered on the airplane, not the pilot.

The airplane was a Long-EZ, a two-seat composite homebuilt of a type designed by Burt Rutan about twenty years ago. The Long-EZ is a canard airplane — its smaller flying surface is in the front and its main wing in the rear — and its engine and propeller are situated in

back, behind the cabin. Fuel is carried in "strakes" —
long wedge-shaped extensions of the wing leading edges
along the sides of the fuselage. The originally intended
powerplants were the Continental 0-200 of 100
horsepower and the Lycoming 0-235 of 115 horsepower,
but many builders install engines of 150 to 180
horsepower.

The proper convention for naming a homebuilt like
Denver's is not to call it a "Rutan Long-EZ" but rather a
Smith Long-EZ or a Jones Long-EZ, depending whether
the original builder was Mr. Smith or Ms. Jones. The
intent is to distinguish the prototype, as designed and
constructed by Rutan and published in his drawings,
from the homemade copies, some of which incorporate
inadvertent deviations from the plans or modifications
dreamed up by their builders. Juries in liability cases are
among the intended recipients of the message that the
homebuilder, not the original designer, is responsible for
the characteristics of particular airplanes.

News reports of the accident provided sketchy
information, but enough to launch rumors. Denver had
been flying at low altitude — a few hundred feet —
above the Pacific near Monterey when his airplane dove
steeply into the water a short distance offshore. At least
twenty people witnessed the accident. As usual their
accounts varied in detail, but the salient points were that
the airplane had been headed westward, that it had
pitched slightly nose up, then dived, and that it was
turned or banked steeply to the right. There had been a

reduction in engine noise before the dive. Some, but not all, described hearing a loud report, like a backfire.

Within days of the accident additional details emerged. The airplane had recently been repainted. There were numerous birds in the area. Denver had had an alcohol abuse problem and his license had been suspended. When the airplane and the victim were recovered from thirty feet of water, we learned that feathers had been found in the wreckage, and that — very surprisingly — the airplane had hit the bottom with sufficient force to break rocks. Hangar-talk theories to account for the accident now included a bird strike, canard flutter, and suicide.

The National Transportation Safety Board published its report in January. As is often the case, its findings bear little resemblance to the scenarios of the theorists. The bird feathers came from a cushion, the canard did not leave the aircraft, and Denver was not intoxicated or despondent.

The crux of the Board's analysis is the location of the fuel tank selector in the airplane. The standard location called out in Rutan's design is at the center of the instrument panel, right in front of the pilot. The builder of this EZ — Denver was its third owner — had been concerned about running fuel lines through the cockpit, however, and had placed the fuel valve behind the firewall, in the engine compartment. The stem of the valve protruded through the firewall, and an aluminum tube four feet long served as an extension to bring the selector handle within reach of the pilot. Only barely within reach, however; it was behind his left shoulder, and, because of the narrowness of the cockpit, the pilot had to turn on the autopilot, let go of the stick (which is located on the right armrest), and reach over his left shoulder with his with his right hand to grasp the selector handle.

The handle positions, furthermore, were not intuitive. When the handle pointed to the right the left tank was selected; when it pointed downward the right tank was selected; and when it pointed upward fuel was shut off. There were no markings, moreover, to indicate the significance of the different selector positions.

The Long-EZ uses sight gauges to indicate fuel quantity; a red float on a column of fuel in a transparent tube indicates the height of the fuel in the tank. The sight gauges are in the sidewalls of the rear cockpit. (Although the NTSB report says that the gauges are visible only to the rear seat occupant, I believe that the pilot can see them if he turns his head.) The sight gauge readings are not linear; that is, the fraction of the gauge height at which the float sits is not the same as the fraction of total fuel that remains in the tank. The gauges in Denver's EZ had no markings, however, to indicate what the float position really meant.

While the fuel system in this particular airplane may seem peculiar, it was all quite legal, because there are virtually no restrictions upon the practices of amateur builders. Furthermore, the airplane had logged 850 hours since it was originally licensed in 1987, and this number — pretty high for a homebuilt — could be seen an empirical proof that whatever the quirks of the fuel system, it could be safely operated by a pilot who understood it. Nevertheless, two pilots who had flown the airplane reported that they had inadvertently run a tank dry "with nearly catastrophic consequences" because of the fuel selector and sight gauge locations.

NTSB investigators inspected another Long-EZ, and found that if they twisted around to reach behind their left shoulder, they inadvertently pressed down on the right rudder pedal. The Long-EZ's swept wings provide strong yaw-roll coupling, and the witnesses' description of a slight pitch up followed by a right roll and a dive is consistent with a sudden, unintentional application of right rudder.

The day before the accident, a pilot who was familiar with the Long-EZ had given Denver a 30-minute checkout at Santa Maria, where the airplane had been repainted. The checkout included slow flight and two touch-and-go landings. Denver had then ferried the airplane to Monterey. He did not refuel it before the accident flight; he said that he only intended to fly for an hour. A mechanic who helped him move the airplane out of the hangar told him — based on the assumption that the sight gauges were linear — that he had "less than half in the right tank and less than a quarter in the left." In

fact, reconstruction of the probable fuel consumption
since the airplane was last refueled at Santa Maria
suggested that between three and six gallons were
aboard. The mechanic noticed that Denver, who flew
with a pillow behind him so that he could reach the
rudder pedals, had difficulty reaching the fuel selector
handle. He lent the singer a mirror so that he could see
the sight gauges as he flew.

After taking off from Monterey, Denver made three
touch-and-go landings in the space of 26 minutes. He
then departed straight out. The accident occurred
moments later. It appeared most likely to the NTSB that
the tank feeding the engine had run dry, and that while
attempting to switch tanks Denver had lost control of the
airplane.

The probable cause, the Board said, was "the pilot's
diversion of attention from the operation of the airplane
and his inadvertent application of right rudder that
resulted in the loss of airplane control while attempting
to manipulate the fuel selector handle." "The pilot's
inadequate preflight planning and preparation,
specifically his failure to refuel the airplane," was also
"causal." Merely "factors in the accident," but not causal,
were "the builder's decision to locate the unmarked fuel
selector handle in a hard-to-access position, unmarked
fuel quantity sight gauges, inadequate transition training
by the pilot, and his lack of total experience in this type
of airplane."

The mechanic who helped Denver prepare for his last flight observed his preflight preparations, which must have been thorough, since he devoted 20 minutes to them. The mechanic did not see Denver visually check the fuel level in his tanks, but he may have done so, and most likely he did. Because the Long-EZ parks in kowtow position with its nose gear retracted, however, and the fuel filler openings are at the rear edge of the tanks, some experience is required to judge how much fuel remains in a partially empty tank.

Evidently, the accident would not have occurred if Denver had refueled before flying. It's never a good idea to take off with minimum fuel, even for a short flight; you never know what problem might arise that will keep you in the air longer than you expect. But a more fundamental issue here has to do with the quality of information Denver had available to him. He did not know with certainty how much fuel was in the airplane; he must have known, however, that it was not a lot. He did not know what was in each tank. He cannot have accepted at face value the mechanic's report that the right tank was a bit under half full and the left under a quarter, since that would have meant that he had used no fuel on the hour-long flight from Santa Maria to Monterey. He had, really, no more than a general idea that there was *some* fuel in the airplane.

Denver had already made arrangements to have his fuel system revised, presumably to the standard arrangement, while he was next on tour. He was aware that it was not ideal; he did not realize that it could be lethal.

No More Dawns

In October, 2006, The National Transportation Safety Board published a "Safety Alert" regarding the need of IFR pilots to "actively maintain awareness of severe weather along their route of flight." This message would hardly seem to require a special publication — What else is new? one might ask — except that it was actually a polite disguise for a quite different warning to airmen: that controllers could not always be relied upon to let pilots know when they were headed for trouble.

The Board cited four recent accidents in which airplanes had crashed after flying into extremely powerful thunderstorms. In each case, the pilot was on an IFR flight plan, was fully qualified and well equipped, had obtained a preflight weather briefing and was in radio communication with controllers. In each case, controllers' radar had painted the storms, their potential severity was known, the airplane was headed straight toward them, and the controllers had said nothing.

The airplanes involved were a Cessna 182 (June 20, 2005, over the Gulf of Mexico off Naples, Florida); a Cessna 210A (April 19, 2006, at Ludville, Georgia); a Mooney M20J (July 26, 2006, at Newellton, Louisiana); and a Mitsubishi MU-2 (September 1, 2006, at Argyle, Florida). It is noteworthy that all four occurred in the South, indicating not necessarily that air traffic controllers there are particularly torpid, but that severe storms are particularly common.

The Ludville, Georgia accident stands out on two accounts. One was the identity of the victim, about which more later. The other was the fact that in that instance, alone among the four, the NTSB cited the action, or lack of it, by the controller as a "probable cause" rather than a "contributing factor," which would have implied a lesser level of culpability. This may seem a minor verbal distinction, and one can often disagree with the Board's assessment of degrees of responsibility, but it is unusual for the Board to identify a controller's omission as the probable cause of a fatal accident.

The 84-year-old, 9,000-hour commercial pilot had obtained several DUAT weather briefings before the flight from Prattville, Alabama to Manassas, Virginia, the last at 7:00 a.m. on the morning of the flight. The information he received included a forecast of thunderstorms along his route. He mentioned to an acquaintance that he "might need to work his way around some weather, but it did not look serious."

Two hours later, the National Weather Service was predicting that a squall line that lay to the north of and parallel to his route, and was moving southward at 35 knots, was likely to develop severe and massively rotating "supercell" thunderstorms with hail, damaging high winds, and possible tornadoes. By the time of the accident, convective SIGMETs were warning of the potential of heavy hail, 60-knot gusts, severe to extreme turbulence, severe icing, and microbursts. Tops in the system would eventually reach 46,000 feet.

The pilot was in contact with Atlanta Center while this rather alarming weather picture was developing. He was probably able to see massive buildups to the left of his course and ahead of him. He did not request updated weather advisories and the controller did not offer them, although traffic was light and the controller was working just one other airplane. All the while, the Stormscope-equipped 210 was flying straight toward a blob of magenta on the controller's radar — a cell of level six, or extreme, intensity.

As the Cessna's radar target reached the center of the cell, the pilot called the controller to request permission to deviate southward for weather. The controller approved the request, and noted that the flight's Mode C readout was 11,500 feet, 500 feet above its assigned altitude.

In the next half-minute, the airplane dropped 6,000 feet before disappearing from radar. The wreckage was found the next day in remote, rugged terrain about three and a half miles northwest of Ludville. Parts reached the ground in two separate groups, a pattern consistent with "low altitude in-flight breakup." Usually when wings fail it is possible to say that they failed upward or downward, but in this case the wings had failed "in various directions," and the wing leading edges were found, together with the left cabin door, eight tenths of a mile from the fuselage and wing spars. The condition of the wreckage was suggestive of unimaginably violent turbulence.

Interviewed by the NTSB, the controller defended his failure to advise the pilot of the dangerous weather in his path on the grounds that "displayed weather can be between six and 15 minutes old and is widely viewed as being unreliable."

"Pilots," he added, "have a better idea of where adverse weather is" than controllers do, and he "expects them to inform him on what actions they need to take to avoid it."

The Board thought differently. The controller, it said, had failed to heed several paragraphs of the FAA order, 7110.65, that governs ATC operations. While weather advisories are of a lower order of priority than traffic conflicts, controllers have a duty, workload permitting, to inform pilots of "pertinent" weather and of its location and intensity. Furthermore, controllers are expected to "plan ahead and be prepared to suggest, at the pilot's request, alternative routes/altitudes."

At the same time, if the pilot could see the squall line on his left it would have been reasonable for him to inquire about it; and if he could not see it because he was flying in clouds, he should have taken pains to inform himself about conditions ahead. While it may be the controller's duty to advise pilots of dangerous weather, it is also a pilot's duty to know everything in his power that pertains to the safety of his flight.

The pilot in this accident was Scott Crossfield. He is little known today, but when I was a boy Crossfield was as mythic a figure to me as Lindbergh or Wiley Post, partly, perhaps, because of his euphonious name (he habitually omitted his first name, which was Albert). As a NASA test pilot in the 1950s he had flown most of the early jet- and rocket-powered X planes. He was the first person to fly twice the speed of sound. He had left NASA to join North American Aviation at the start of the X-15 program, and was the test pilot for the magnificent rocket plane's early — and often trouble-plagued — flights. More than a test pilot, he was an aerodynamicist and engineer who was probably largely responsible for the excellent flying qualities of the X-15. After leaving North American in 1967, Crossfield held a series of distinguished positions in aviation which included advising the Congressional Committee on Science and Technology, from which he retired in 1993.

It happened that I read Crossfield's autobiography, *Always Another Dawn*, several months after his accident. If Crossfield's CV was impressive, it became more so when one read the book — written, somewhat prematurely, in the late 1960s with the help of a ghost writer, military historian Clay Blair Jr. — in which he emerged as a thoughtful, resourceful, courageous, feeling and funny man whose ego seemed admirably free of bloat. He didn't mind telling a good story at his own expense. One involved an incident, after the War, when he was part of an exhibition squadron of Corsairs. The flight left Montana for Denver, but, because of lackadaisical navigation and a general feeling on each pilot's part that someone else in the group must know where they were, they first got lost and then got separated from one another. Crossfield's small contingent, confronted with failing light, a wall of black thunderclouds along a mountain ridge, and just half an hour's fuel left in their tanks, finally capitulated to common sense and landed at a small airfield somewhere in the sticks. The next morning they learned that they were only 23 miles from Denver, and could have made it if they'd just pressed on for another six minutes.

Their commanding officer flew down from Seattle to chew them out. "I can understand one plane, or maybe two planes, getting lost," he said. "By really stretching my imagination I can conceive of maybe six planes getting lost together. But fifteen airplanes, in largely clear weather on a four-hundred-mile flight! An hour-and-a-half hop. It's beyond belief."

Crossfield ended that chapter with a reflection that it is probably unfair to bring up now — it's like convicting someone of murder because in a heated moment long ago he had exclaimed, "I'd like to kill that son of a bitch!" — but the irony is too poignant to be allowed to pass unnoticed.

"Not once since then, either on land or in the air," Crossfield wrote, "have I ever turned back from any course that I set upon, no matter how dark the clouds that lay ahead."

The Hazard of Ox

If you've ever been troubled by doubts about the
plausibility of Dorothy's being carried off in her house by
a tornado and then dumped back on the ground, house
and all, without injury to herself or Toto, an accident that
took place a few years ago should set your mind at rest.

A Cessna 337D Skymaster, an unpressurized,
turbocharged twin that had been modified with a floor-
mounted camera in the cabin, departed its home base in
order to do some aerial photography. The owner, a
3,100-hour private pilot, and his assistant were aboard.
After photographing three locations, they landed at
another airport. There the pilot filed an IFR flight plan
and "set up" the portable oxygen system, which had been
charged that morning, for the next flight. This time, they
would be climbing to 25,000 feet.

They took off at quarter to two. As they climbed through 10,000 feet, the pilot told his assistant to put her oxygen mask on. He did the same. The assistant tried to turn on the oxygen but wasn't sure how, and the pilot reached back to open the valve. The assistant knew the oxygen was now on, because she could feel cool air flowing into the mask and the flow indicator ring in the oxygen line changed from red to green.

As the Skymaster climbed through 20,000 feet, the pilot remarked on the altitude and asked the assistant how she was doing and whether she felt OK. She said she did. Then, however, she became aware that she was starting to feel dizzy and was having trouble focusing. She felt as though she were cross-eyed. She said to the pilot that she was feeling dizzy, but he didn't respond. He must be talking to the tower, she thought. She closed her eyes and noticed that this made her feel better.

Air Traffic Control had cleared the flight to maintain FL 250. Controllers, unable to communicate with the pilot, observed the airplane climbing through that altitude, eventually reaching 27,700 feet. It then descended to 26,000 feet before radar contact was lost.

Shortly afterward, the airplane rained down in pieces over an area of several square miles. Both tail booms, together with the empennage, outboard left wing and the right door, had separated from the cabin, which fluttered down with its two occupants inside and came to rest 30 feet above the ground in a hickory tree. The pilot was dead, not from the impact but from lack of oxygen. His assistant, however, was merely unconscious. Perhaps benefiting from the divine protection said to be accorded to some who collide with doors, stairs and lampposts while in states of impaired consciousness, she sustained only cuts and bruises in the crash.

The weather at the time of the accident was good, and there was no indication of any mechanical malfunction. Investigators tested the gas in the FBO's oxygen bottle from which the portable unit had been filled, and found it to be not pure oxygen but, instead, simply compressed air. It appeared that, because of some misunderstanding between the FBO and his oxygen supplier, the FBO had been regularly receiving, and dispensing, compressed air in the belief that it was aviator's breathing oxygen.

A bottle of compressed air is useful at sea level (for breathing in toxic environments, for example) and under water, but it is of no use at all at high altitude, because once the air emerges from the bottle it is at ambient pressure and is no different, for breathing purposes, from the surrounding air.

Atmospheric air consists mostly of nitrogen, a gas having no role in human metabolism. Only 21 percent of it is oxygen. What counts for maintaining the required level of oxygen in the blood is the so-called "partial pressure" of the oxygen in the air being breathed. The body's uptake of oxygen is proportionate to both the ambient pressure, which is a fraction of sea level pressure, and the fraction of the breathed gas that is oxygen; in fact, it is proportionate to the product of the two fractions.

The whole point of feeding bottled oxygen into a mask is to create around the user's nose and mouth a little island of air that is abnormally rich in oxygen, and thus to preserve a more or less constant partial pressure at the same time as the ambient pressure is decreasing. An atmosphere containing 42 percent oxygen, or double the normal concentration, breathed at a pressure altitude of 18,000 feet, is equivalent, for the body's purposes, to a sea level atmosphere, because at 18,000 feet atmospheric pressure is half what it is at sea level.

That different people are differently affected by hypoxia is grimly evident in the fact that the pilot-photographer died (according to the autopsy) from lack of oxygen while at altitude, while his assistant merely slept. Most people operate at altitudes of 5,000 to 7,000 feet without experiencing any of the uncomfortable symptoms, including headache, nausea and vertigo, referred to as "altitude sickness." Individuals differ, some tolerating altitude better than others, but many pilots routinely cruise at 10,000 feet, where the pressure is 70 percent of the sea level value, without using oxygen and without displaying any hypoxic symptoms, and FAR 91.211 requires oxygen use (after 30 minutes) only at 12.500 feet (where the pressure is about 62 percent of the sea level value) and above. The regulations, by the way, make no distinction between smokers and non-smokers,

although it is well established that smokers are more
prone to hypoxia.

Charts of physiological effects of altitude are widely
available but do not agree with one another, some
speaking merely of "time of useful consciousness" at
altitudes near 30,000 feet, others of imminent death.
Mount Everest, 29,000 feet high, has been climbed a
number of times without oxygen. Climbers, of course,
adapt to high altitudes, spending weeks camped at 18,000
feet before finally assaulting the peak. But the mere fact
that some people die in a few minutes at 29,000 feet
while others trudge up a very steep mountain shows the
extreme variability of human types, physical conditions
and reactions to hypoxia, and also seems to suggest that
the same person may react differently to it at different
times.

Although the assistant, who survived to describe her
sensations, had noticed that she was feeling strange as
the airplane climbed through 20,000 feet, the pilot
evidently succumbed without suspecting anything. The
belief that you are breathing oxygen would tend to dispel
any doubts, but one of the effects of hypoxia (as is also
the case with alcohol) is a happy, confident feeling that
undermines whatever concerns a pilot might normally
experience when feeling dizzy or having blurred vision
or blue fingernails, and makes him cheerfully forgiving
of his own mistakes. It's a fair bet, since aviators'
breathing oxygen is expensive and not available
everywhere, charging onboard systems is time-

consuming, and most airplanes that are capable of climbing to oxygen altitudes (which is to say, most airplanes) don't have oxygen systems, that many pilots have flirted with hypoxia and continue doing so without being aware of it. Normally, cruising flight places so few demands on a pilot's physical and intellectual skills that we are able to perform adequately even when chronically, if mildly, hypoxic.

A pilot needn't rely on guesswork to know his oxygen state. Pulse oximeters, which report the amount of oxygen in the blood in terms of a percentage of its total carrying capacity, are inexpensive and readily available. Their use is simple: you stick a finger into the device and wait a few seconds for a reading to appear, along with your pulse rate (a less useful piece of information), on the display. Normal oxygen saturation is 95 to 99 percent; a reading below 90 percent should be cause for concern if you're doing anything more demanding than washing your dog.

Considering the cost of aviators' breathing oxygen (which comes in green bottles so labeled, not yellow ones from which the Skymaster's system was charged), an oximeter will quickly pay for itself in oxygen saved. Having no way to judge how much oxygen is enough, pilots and passengers who use oxygen probably use more than they need. A pulse oximeter is a perfect method of regulating consumption and extending the range of an oxygen bottle.

Incidentally, it is not clear that there is any longer a significant difference between aviators' breathing oxygen, medical oxygen and welding oxygen. Aviators' oxygen supposedly contains less moisture, which could become an issue in systems plumbed through unheated parts of an airplane, where moisture might freeze, blocking flow. That may have been the case decades ago. But modern oxygen distillation systems yield pure, dry oxygen for all purposes; in fact, in hospitals the oxygen is re-moisturized (bypassing it through a sort of bong) on the way to the cannula to avoid dehydrating the patient's mucous membranes.

Hypoxia is a nebulous threat. It may be a factor in many more pilot errors than we know, but to place it unequivocally in a chain of accident causation is usually difficult. In this case, however, its role was obvious, and extreme: it actually killed the pilot.

One aspect of this accident that is worth noting, though it has nothing to do with oxygen, is that the unpiloted airplane broke apart in flight. Presumably, this happened because it picked up sufficient speed in a spiral dive for some part to flutter. It is customary, when an airplane breaks apart in flight, especially after a VFR pilot has flown into a cloud, to attribute the breakup to some pilot action, such as a desperate pull-out that overstresses the wings. This accident demonstrates that no pilot action is needed; left to its own devices, an airplane may go into a spiral dive and eventually break up all by itself.

Close Encounters

Chen Keyue is lucky.

Mr. Chen, a Chinese national and a student at an Arizona flight academy, was on an instrument practice flight with a fellow student, Feng Shuai, in a Cessna 152. Both were private pilots with about 160 hours. Mr. Feng was in the left seat and was flying, and Mr. Chen was in the right. They were returning to their base after a series of touch-and-gos at another airport when they collided with a Cherokee that was also on a training flight. The Cherokee landed under control in a field with minimal damage to its airframe or occupants, but the impact severed the tail and much of the right wing of the Cessna. The pilot of the 152 was ejected as what was left of the airplane fell, inverted, to the ground. Mr. Chen remained strapped in his seat. He awoke to find someone cutting his seatbelt in order to extricate him from the wreckage.

Interviewed several days later, Mr Chen could remember little about the accident or the moments preceding it, but he believed that he had been making position reports on the radio. He did not see the Cherokee, either before or after the collision. Investigators were uncertain whether he was suffering from traumatic amnesia, which is not uncommon, or was reluctant to talk because, as an interviewer wrote, "In China, when government officials show up, it's not pleasant for anyone involved."

The midair collision involving Mr. Chen was unusual in that three of the four persons involved survived. Midairs are not always so merciful, but there are survivors more often than you might imagine. There were seven midairs in the United States during 2009, according to National Transportation Safety Board records; they took 19 lives and left 7 survivors. (Oddly, three of these collisions took place, respectively, on 8/8/09, 9/9/09, and 10/10/09; numerologists, take note.)

Two of them involved formation flying of a somewhat impromptu kind. In one case, two Cessna 150's were flying together, in radio contact and with one at the other's 5 o'clock position. The lead airplane made a sudden right turn; the trailing pilot tried to avoid the collision but could not. Both airplanes crashed; both occupants of the lead airplane died, while the two occupants of the other survived. The other formation accident involved a homebuilt RV-8 and a Nanchang CJ-6A, a Chinese-built radial-engined trainer that resembles a Yak-52. The sequence of events was broadly similar to those of the other formation accident, except that in this case the lead pilot, who was trained in formation flying, turned gently, and the pilot in trail, whom he could not see, overtook him. A photograph taken at the instant of the collision shows the ailerons of the overtaking RV in a neutral position, while those of the Nanchang are deflected out of turn and its elevators are commanding a pitch-up. The left wing of the RV was severed and it crashed, killing the pilot; the Nanchang landed safely.

People involved in formation flying almost always know one another. Sometimes, however, there are other connections between pilots involved in midair collisions. In one case, a glider approached an airport on a right downwind while the airplane that had towed it aloft approached on the left downwind. Neither saw the other, and they collided as they simultaneously turned to final. Both pilots were killed. In another strange instance, two small sporting aircraft, one of them a "powered parachute" and the other an ultralight, operating at twilight from neighboring grass strips belonging to the respective pilots, collided as the powered parachute was approaching to land and the ultralight was making a final circuit of the area before landing. The pilot of the powered parachute died; the ultralight crashed, but the pilot survived.

On a late afternoon in May, a Cessna 172 on an instructional flight was maneuvering in a practice area south of Long Beach, California, when it collided with a

Cessna 310 moving at high speed. The sun was low, and another pilot, flying southward at the same altitude and keeping the 172 in view on his left, noticed the 310 coming from the west. "Due to its speed I believed it to be a twin engine," he reported, "but could not make out the outline because the sun was almost at the horizon and I could only make out a black object moving." He saw the impact. "The debris rained down, much like when a firework goes off in the sky, in small pieces."

The most notorious midair collision of the year was the one involving a Cherokee Lance and a Eurocopter AS350 over the Hudson River. The Lance, which had taken off from Teterboro and was bound for Ocean City, New Jersey, was flying down the Hudson at 1,100 feet in order to remain clear of Class B; the pilot had requested VFR flight following, but was between controllers when the collision occurred. The Lance overtook the AS350 from its 5 o'clock; amateur video of the collision suggests that the Lance pilot made an attempt to veer away to the right, but only a split-second before the collision.

Seven accidents form too small a sample to allow one to draw broad conclusions about midair collisions in general. Nevertheless, it is worthwhile to notice some of their common features.

In four of the seven accidents, the pilots involved knew one another; those collisions all took place in the vicinity of airports or landing fields, and in three of the four at least one of the pilots had the other in sight or knew him to be in the vicinity. Only in the case of the glider that collided with its own tow plane on final approach did neither pilot have reason to expect the other to be where it was at that moment.

In the other three cases, the collisions took place in areas known for their heavy traffic — the Hudson corridor and practice areas near Phoenix and Long Beach. These were places where pilots had reason to be particularly vigilant. In two of the three collisions, one aircraft overtook the other; the speed difference between them cannot have been very large, and so the overtaking pilot must have had the other airplane in his field of view for more than a second or two before the collision. Only the collision between the 310 and the 172 near Long Beach involved airplanes whose tracks were perpendicular to one another and whose closure rate, possibly over 175 knots, meant that they were conspicuous to one another for only a few seconds before the collision.

The FAR relevant to midair collisions is Part 91, Section 113. Basically, it says that all pilots (even those flying IFR) must maintain "vigilance" so as to "see and avoid" other aircraft, and it lays down some simple rules concerning right of way. The NTSB, in determining the "probable cause" of a midair collision (probable causes have not yet been issued for several of 2009's collisions), seems to assume that failure to avoid a collision implies either a failure of vigilance or a violation of right-of-way rules, or both. For example, it attributed the collision of the RV-8 and the Nanchang to "both pilots' failure to maintain adequate clearance from each other in the airport traffic pattern" although the pilot of the Nanchang evidently did not see the RV and did not know, until it overtook him, exactly where it was.

It's unlikely that right-of-way has much to do with midair collisions. Airplanes don't collide because they disagree about their rights; they collide because they fail to notice one another. The NTSB seems to assume that a collision is prima facie proof of a lack of vigilance; but it would be more reasonable to recognize that vigilance, though it seems to work most of the time, is not perfectly reliable. Looking is not the same thing as seeing, and, more subtly, seeing is not the same thing as recognizing. The human brain is not a perfect analyst of the seen world. In cluttered visual environments, or when the airplane on a collision course is converging rapidly or is coming out of the sun, even a vigilant pilot cannot be sure of detecting every threat.

Many animal species would not exist if it were not possible to hide in plain sight; and the paint schemes on most airplanes — stripes that tend to break up the overall outline — are a fair approximation of camouflage. Most pilots have at one time or another in their careers been startled to suddenly spot an airplane passing by quite close to them, and have wondered how they could have failed to notice it earlier. And we have all certainly had a target called out to us by a controller, and have persistently failed to see it, even though we knew where to look, until we finally heard the words "no longer a factor."

All-nighter

It's seldom that one of the National Transportation Safety Board's accident narratives rises to the artistic level of, say, a chapter in a noir novel. Here is one that does.

The accident took place on Independence Day, 1993, at Prescott, Arizona, a little after three in the morning. Its prelude began earlier that night, when a Cessna T303 Crusader light twin landed at Prescott an hour before midnight. Three men emerged from the airplane, one of them clutching a can of beer. A fueler greeted them and asked if they needed any gasoline. "Not right now, maybe later or in the morning," one of the men replied. They were meeting friends, they said, and did not need a place to stay.

One of them called his girlfriend to ask for a ride to "downtown" Prescott — the quotation marks are the NTSB's — and she came to the airport. As the men were walking to the entrance of the airport to meet her, the manager of a nearby motel saw them drinking some beverage from cans; the girl friend later reported that these were, in fact, beer cans. She took them into town and dropped them off around midnight, with plans to meet later.

The three men disappear from our screens for an hour. Then, at around one a.m., they approach three women leaving the Palace Saloon. One of the men identifies himself as a pilot — an irresistible pickup line, as we all know — but one of the women, who has known a pilot or two in her day, does not believe him. "How many hours do you need bottle to throttle?" she asks him. "Eight," replies the pilot. "But I guess I'll have to break that rule tonight."

The six stroll along, conversing. The woman who challenged the pilot now walks beside him. She finds him quiet and friendly; he does not seem intoxicated, and at one point apologizes for not being more amusing. He's tired, he says; last night he was in Laughlin, Nevada, he worked all day, then rented the airplane and flew to Prescott.

They go to a restaurant and eat; then they walk to the women's hotel. There, the men suggest that they drive out to the airport, and the women agree. Two of the men continue chatting during the ride to the airport, but the tired pilot is still quiet, leaning his head back and closing his eyes.

They get to the airport at a quarter to three, and the women come out to look at the airplane. The pilot climbs into the cockpit. The woman who had been walking beside him before now turns to one of the other men. "Why is the pilot so quiet, is he drunk?" she asks. "No," replies the man, "he only had a few drinks."

The other men climb into the airplane, and a discussion follows. The pilot is trying to trigger the airport surface lights by keying his microphone. "Stop clicking the button so many times," the man in the right front seat, also a commercial pilot, says. "It's supposed to be three clicks and then stop."

The men now invite the women to come along for a ten-minute hop around the patch. It's a perfect night for flying: warm, calm, clear.

The woman who had earlier challenged the pilot declines, and goes to wait for her friends in their car; the two other climb into the airplane.

At 2:54, the specialist in the Prescott Flight Service Station receives a call from the pilot of the Cessna saying that he has been unsuccessful in trying to activate the pilot-controlled lights. The specialist tells him that the frequency for activating the lights is 125.3; he then hears seven clicks on his own frequency. "You're still on 122.4," he says. "Thank you sir," comes the reply, "We got 'em."

A little later the specialist contacts the airplane again, and provides the pilot with AIRMET Tango for occasional moderate turbulence below 20,000 feet.

The radar recordings from Albuquerque Center show a single aircraft taking off from Runway 21 at Prescott at 3:19 a.m., climbing to 1,500 agl, and remaining in the pattern.

The woman waiting in the car was the only survivor that night. The pilot died of a fractured skull, the other occupants of broken necks suffered when the airplane, under control, struck the ground hard 2,000 feet short of the runway. The airframe was heavily damaged, but not demolished. The airplane, its fuselage broken in two places, remained standing on the landing gear, which did not collapse, although the wing spar was bent downward between the struts.

The scenario of one or more men going flying after an evening of drinking is not unusual. The bottle-to-throttle rule, obviously familiar to the pilot in this case, is simple enough to understand and apply; but the perilous power of alcohol is not only that it impairs piloting skills, but also that it undermines the drinker's sense of the seriousness of all strictures. The tired, taciturn, brooding pilot announced his intention of breaking the bottle-to-throttle rule as nonchalantly as if it were merely a matter of forgetting to check his messages or take his vitamins.

In fact, neither of the two commercial SMEL/instrument pilots in the front seats was seriously intoxicated; the right-seat pilot's blood alcohol level was 0.01 percent — 0.08 percent is the threshold for a DUI in some states — and the left-seat pilot's was even lower. But the NTSB suggested that the combined effects of altitude — Prescott is at 5,000 feet — alcohol and fatigue could have impaired the pilot's skills.

What may also have complicated the approach was that it was made over dark terrain on a dark night. This is a circumstance that is known to produce powerful visual illusions; even pilots who had had nothing at all to drink and may have been well rested have landed on moonless nights in the ocean behind aircraft carriers, and in the snow thousands of feet short of the runways of wilderness airports, because they believed themselves to be much higher than they were. A sudden wind shear could also have been a factor; although the wind on the surface was only four knots, the area is mountainous, and they had received the AIRMET for turbulence.

Since any of these factors could have caused the accident singly or in various combinations, it's not really necessary to invoke all of them at once. The NTSB does, however. The probable cause reads:

"The pilot misjudging altitude during a night approach. Factors which contributed to the accident were: the pilot's impairment due to fatigue exacerbated by alcohol consumption, the dark night, and the high density altitude and turbulent weather condition."

The NTSB makes no remark about the excellent judgment of the woman who remained behind in the car.

Hold on Tight

There are two kinds of people: those who find spins exhilarating, and those who find them terrifying.

I found them exhilarating when my instructor, Betty Faux, first demonstrated them to me in a Cessna 150 during the course of my post-private-ticket training. I promptly invited friends to share this great thrill. We would fly out over the ocean, climb to 6,000 feet or so, and do spin after spin. It's amazing they didn't all barf.

At the time I had no understanding whatever of the fact that to some people the sensations of a spin are quite frightening. You might replace "some people" in that sentence with "all rational people," because it is really quite natural to experience some anxiety when you are thousands of feet up in the air, the little crate to which you have entrusted your life suddenly keels over into a rapidly gyrating vertical descent, and a quick mental calculation reveals that you have about 15 seconds to live. But I was young and in love with flying, and the fact that you could get an airplane to do something so remote from straight-and-level flight, and that it would instantly, almost magically, recover on your command — why, this seemed absolutely intoxicating.

I later took a two-day spin course in a Pitts from Gene Beggs. The gist of Beggs's doctrine was that an airplane would recover from a spin on its own if you just released the controls. This is not universally true, and I think Beggs knew it, but it was true of enough airplanes — and the ones of which it isn't true you would not be likely to spin — that the hands-off recovery would certainly be worth knowing about when all else fails. I cannot say that I found inverted flat spins in the Pitts quite as pleasant as upright nose-down spins in the 150, but with the aid of a patch of transdermal scopalomine I got through them.

Many spins follow inadvertent stalls, often during botched turns from base to final or during ill-advised attempts to turn back to a runway after an engine failure. But in June, 2006, a deliberate spin, during session of flight school spin training, went terribly wrong, killing both student and instructor. While it is impossible to know exactly what happened to bring this routine flying lesson to a fatal conclusion, I am inclined to guess that an important element was the fact that the student did not see spins as benign and entertaining maneuvers, but rather as close encounters with eternity.

Investigators analyzing the accident interviewed several instructors and students at the student's flight academy, seeking anything that might shed light on the failure of the Cessna 152 — an airplane that does recover by itself if you release the controls — to pull out of its final spin.

Two students recalled doing spin training with the instructor, and reported nothing out of the ordinary. Both had completed the sequence without difficulty and both had discovered that the 152 would recover from a spin of its own accord.

Instructors who had flown with the student pilot, who was taking the multi-engine CFI course, had more light to shed.

One instructor described the student's piloting skills as "lacking" in situations that required piloting "outside the box." The "box" was none too capacious; "stressful" situations that caused the student to act "impulsively" included shutting down an engine or stalling the airplane. This instructor recalled two separate occasions on which the student had "stiffened on the controls, seizing the yoke, as if petrified." On one occasion he had to jab the student in the leg to get him to relax his grip. He reported that the student had asked a great many questions during ground training on spins and had seemed "very nervous" about the future spin flight; but on the morning of the accident he appeared calm and to be "looking forward to the flight."

Another instructor who had worked with the student on his multi-engine commercial certificate recalled "numerous occasions" on which the student acted "impulsively" in reaction to a simulated "stressful situation." In one instance, a stopped engine failed to restart. The student appeared "panicked" and the instructor had to take over the controls. To get the engine windmilling, the instructor pushed the nose over to gain speed. At this, the terrified student grabbed the control yoke and held it "firmly aft." He would not relax his grip until the instructor jabbed him in the leg (leg-jabbing must be a standard technique in certain types of flight instruction).

A pattern emerges. This is a student who does not really believe in airplanes. His anxieties about flying are not far below the surface, and burst out whenever something happens that is not routine and expected. "Below the surface" is a merely metaphorical expression, of course, and does not illuminate anything about the actual mechanisms of barely suppressed anxiety. Rationally, we ask why someone whose confidence in airplanes is so easily shaken wants to become a flight instructor in the first place. The reasons may be complex, but we would not be surprised to see a fearful person enlist in the army. The paradoxical vocation offers, at once, a veneer of bravery for public show and the hope that, through practice and perhaps contagion, real courage will be acquired.

A sudden onset of in-flight anxiety can manifest itself in various ways. The one most of us would consider reasonable is for the student to relinquish control of the airplane to the instructor. "Your airplane" is a magic phrase that solves all problems. But this student had a different, and a more ominous, reaction: He seized the controls and held on for dear life. The annals of flight instruction contain many instances of this death grip. Fear is a great multiplier of strength, and an instructor may be hard pressed to pry a panicked student loose from the controls.

Radar returns recorded by ATC and by a nearby Air Force base sketched out the course of the 40-minute flight. The 152 had climbed to about 6,000 msl on the way to the practice area. It had then performed what appeared to be seven one-turn spins to the left in quick succession. At 1527:24 it was at 5,600 msl, doing 70 knots groundspeed on a 045 heading. It then turned to the east while losing altitude and speed. At 1527:34 it was at 4,600 feet — descending 6,000 fpm — with a groundspeed of 60 knots. Ten seconds later it had made a sharp turn to the right and was northbound at 50 knots, descending through 4,100 feet. Five seconds later it had lost another 900 feet and slowed to 40 knots. The last radar return came five seconds after that: 2,800 feet, 30 knots. The 152 had given up 2,800 feet in 30 seconds. It was then only 650 feet, and seven seconds, from the ground.

100

Some time after the accident, an FAA operations inspector performed a series of one-, two- and three-turn spins. He found that a three-turn spin produced an altitude loss of 2,900 feet in 15 seconds; a two-turn spin lost 1,700 feet in 12 seconds; and a one-turn spin consumed 700 to 800 feet in eight seconds.

The descent chronicled by radar is most consistent with a series of spins interrupted by momentary recoveries. Why this happened only after seven spins had been successfully executed is unclear, but perhaps they were all demonstrations by the instructor. In any case, something was different about the eighth. One imagines the 230-pound student, paralyzed by the sight of the onrushing earth, pulling the yoke back with all his might while the instructor, a 100-pound woman who would certainly not have been able to overpower him, tried frantically with the rudder pedals to gain control of the airplane.

The National Transportation Safety Board's findings of probable cause are often silly, tautological ("the pilot's failure to remain clear of terrain"), or obtuse, but this one is positively idiotic. Choosing to ignore all the evidence presented in its own accident report — including evidence that it is practically impossible *not* to recover from a spin in a 152 — the Board blames the accident on "the failure of both the flight instructor and student pilot to regain control of the airplane in a timely manner during an intentional spin maneuver ... A factor ... was the instructor's inadequate supervision of the flight."

It Hasn't Killed Me Yet

The pilot, 69, had almost finished a 6-month refurbishment of a Piper PA-12 Super Cruiser. He had been rebuilding airplanes for 40 years, and his habit was to have a certain A&P mechanic perform a "semi-final" inspection as each project neared completion. The mechanic would give him a list of things that needed to be done before he could sign the airplane off. According to the mechanic, it often happened that before he returned to perform the final inspection the pilot would already have performed a "fast taxi test." This "test" typically went well beyond the usual understanding of taxiing: The pilot would accelerate, lift off, fly along the runway a few feet above the ground, and then set down. The mechanic objected to this practice and had repeatedly scolded the pilot for it, pointing out that it was not just illegal but also unsafe. The pilot's insouciant

102

reply, with a shrug and a big smile, was that he had done it many times and it hadn't killed him yet.

This time — it was near the end of September in 2009 — the mechanic was not available to look at the airplane when the pilot called him. He suggested a subsequent weekend, but the pilot did not want to wait; he said that he would look for another inspector, and if he couldn't find one he would call back. He didn't call, and to all appearances didn't find another inspector either.

On Thursday, October 8, a little before noon, the pilot asked a couple of men at a nearby hangar whether they would mind helping him. They gladly went with him to his hangar, where one held a piece of aluminum tubing which the pilot, after removing an access cover on top of the wing, attached to the fuel tank vent. After finishing the small task, the three chatted amiably for a while, the pilot telling the others about this airplane and the many others he had restored. He said that his project for the day was to test-run his recently overhauled engine. The airplane was not, indeed, ready for flight; the two visitors noted many unsecured panels and other items still incomplete.

The two returned to their hangar, and about 15 minutes later they heard the Super Cruiser's engine start. It ran for several minutes at a moderate power setting, without any variation that might suggest a mag or carb heat check, before shutting down. Another 15 minutes passed, and they then heard the engine start again. This time, they were surprised to see the Super Cruiser taxi out to the runway and into position.

The engine went to what sounded like full power, and after a short takeoff roll the airplane became airborne. Its nose pitched up steeply and it climbed to a height of 150 or 200 feet, its engine still at high power, before dropping off to the right into a nearly vertical dive and crashing alongside the runway. It bounced once and came to rest on its back in the grass, its front end and the leading edges of its wings crushed. The pilot died from the impact.

One of the routine tests performed by NTSB accident investigators is the control continuity check. It very seldom happens that controls become disconnected in flight, but cables often break during a crash and so investigators look for the "broom straw" signature that indicates a sudden tension overload as opposed to, say, gradual abrasion or a saboteur's neat cut. In this case, although the crash impact had separated the propeller and its mounting flange from the crankshaft, the airplane had remained more or less in one piece — it was later towed back to a hangar on its wheels — and the investigator in charge was able to move all of the control surfaces from the cockpit. He quickly uncovered the cause of the accident: The connections of the control cables to the elevator bellcrank were reversed. Forward movement of the stick raised the trailing edge of the elevator; pulling the stick back lowered it.

The accident sequence is easy to imagine. As is customary in taildraggers, the pilot would have begun the takeoff roll with the stick back. As the airplane gained speed, he would have pushed the stick forward to lift the tail. Because the pitch control was reversed, however, forward stick merely held the tail down, and, before the pilot could reflect on the oddity of the tail failing to rise, the airplane, light in weight and accelerating, leaped into the air. At this point, startled by the suddenness with which he found himself airborne and by the airplane's persistent nose-high attitude, the pilot, who had 3,500 hours and was no stranger to taildraggers, would instinctively have pushed the stick farther forward. But this produced exactly the opposite of the intended effect: The nose pointed to the sky, and the airplane struggled upward toward an inevitable stall. There was no time to think about what was happening or to reason that the airplane's perverse response to pitch control could mean only one thing. When it left the ground, the airplane's fate was sealed.

The mechanic who had inspected previous airplanes for the pilot provided a written statement to the FAA in which he reported that he had found improperly connected controls on two previous projects of his: reversed ailerons on a Cessna 170 and a reversed elevator on a Piper Cub. (Reversed ailerons have killed many test pilots, but a very few have burnished their legends by correctly analyzing the problem once airborne and using reversed roll controls to return for a safe landing.) He also remarked that investigators were not likely to find a log recording the details of the rebuild because the pilot "was sort of anti towards the FAA and FAA regulations."

This accident inspires many reflections. One is that in a perfect world engineers would routinely design critical control systems in such a way that they cannot be inadvertently mis-rigged; there are many ways to achieve this, none of them difficult or expensive. Another is that one ought to take one's own mistakes to heart. This pilot-rebuilder had made the same type of mistake twice before, and would probably have been killed on one of the earlier occasions but for the intervention of his mechanic. One would expect such close calls to make a deep impression; but they apparently did not.

Another lesson is that, especially after maintenance, pilots ought to check the controls not only for freedom but also for movement in the appropriate directions. In fact, all control checks, before every flight, should be done with this same consciousness of purpose, even in airplanes that have not been recently maintained or ones whose pushrod controls cannot be improperly connected. The reason to force oneself to consciously interrogate each control — right turn, left aileron goes down, right one goes up etc etc — even when there is no possibility of its misbehaving is to ensure that one does not sink gradually into that state of checklist hypnosis where habitual responses and conditioned expectations erase all awareness of what is actually going on before our eyes. In this case, the pilot obviously either did not check the controls or else he checked them without consciously reflecting upon what they were doing. So insidious is the force of habit and expectation that it should be the policy of everyone preparing an airplane for its first flight, or for a test flight after re-assembly, to have a second person look the airplane over.

The NTSB noted that the pilot suffered from a chronic itchy skin condition — urticaria, or hives — and that the autopsy had disclosed the presence of an "impairing antihistamine" in his system. It was possible, the NTSB commented in its report, that while the airplane could probably not have been controlled once airborne, "impairment from the use of diphenhydramine or distraction from chronic urticaria [could have] contributed to the pilot's failure to correctly rig the elevator cables."

Still, unlike an omission during a preflight inspection or a misjudgment made in flight, this error did not involve a single momentary distraction. The pilot knew about mis-rigging; he had done it twice before. It is natural to test the action of the controls after connecting them, and to test them again before a first flight. There had been many opportunities for the pilot himself to catch the error. That the A&P who had performed many inspections for the pilot reported that he "generally found many things wrong" suggests a pattern of inattention and overconfidence. That he was "sort of anti" toward the FAA and its regulations also implies a failure, not uncommon in these days of discontent, to distinguish between government and the law. However annoying and heavy-handed the FAA may sometimes be in the enforcement of its rules, the rules themselves, or at least most of them, represent the distilled experience of a century of flight. Independent-minded pilots need to find a safe path between the rule-bound and the devil-may-care. This wasn't it.

Almost There

The distance from Campbell Airport (C81), a little north of Chicago, to Saint Petersburg-Clearwater International (PIE) in Florida is about 920 nautical miles.

A Piper PA-28-181 Archer has two 25-gallon tanks, but is officially credited with 48 gallons of usable fuel. The handbook says that at 75 percent power and best-power mixture, it burns 10.5 gallons an hour and cruises at 125 knots. The required fuel reserve for night VFR is 45 minutes at a "normal" power setting. Since a more conservative setting than max cruise certainly qualifies as normal, the reserve might arguably be six gallons. In addition, some extra fuel is required for taxi, runup, and climb; let's say 1.5 gallons.

Question: Ignoring wind, how would you plan a trip from C81 to PIE?

This is the kind of problem that might be presented to a student preparing for the private license. The arithmetic is simple. Although in level, coordinated flight you probably have access to almost the whole 50 gallons, we'll go by the book and start with 48. Subtract 1.5 for taxi and climb and six for reserve. That leaves you 40.5 gallons. Divide by 10.5 gph, and you can fly for three hours and 50 minutes, covering about 480 nm.

So you could make the trip in two legs, provided that one was not shorter than 440 nm (because 440+480=920). Or you could make two stops, in which case leg length would be of less concern. Or you could lean the mixture and slow down to, say, 115 knots. That would reduce your fuel flow to around eight gph and prolong the flight by 40 minutes, but it would increase your maximum leg length by 100 nm.

Such was the calculation that presented itself to a father who intended to take his 15-year-old daughter and her best friend from chilly Illinois to toasty Florida for their spring break. The 53-year-old businessman, a 1,600-hour pilot and, according to an obituary, a "larger than life" figure and pillar of his community and church, had owned the Archer for seven years and probably had a pretty good idea of what it could and couldn't do — including some notion of how the fuel gauges behaved. The Archer, not lightning-fast, would require at least seven hours and 20 minutes to cover the distance. Throw in a meal or two and the time to refuel and stretch your legs, and just getting to Florida and back was going to eat up two days of the nine-day vacation.

Perhaps it was with that in mind that he decided — or *they* decided, since his daughter liked to call herself his copilot — to leave Friday night, fly all night, and be in Florida to greet the semitropical sun. It was an ambitious plan, and could be pretty exhausting for all aboard; and so it was perhaps natural that the pilot might choose to cruise at 75% of power and best-power mixture.

What was harder to understand was why he made the first stop at Nashville, after flying only 366 nm, 74 nm short of the minimum leg length for a one-stop trip. He now had either to throttle back and slow down, or to make a second en route stop.

He did neither. Instead, at four in the morning, after four hours and 21 minutes airborne, he ran out of fuel six miles short of PIE. He tried to land on a broad, well-lighted highway, and would most likely have succeeded had an unlucky set of high tension lines 160 feet above the road not gotten in the way. The crash killed the pilot and his daughter; the other girl, although seriously injured, survived.

There can be many reasons for running low on fuel sooner than expected: headwinds that prolong a flight, tailwinds that make you optimistically skip a planned stop, tanks not filled to the brim, too rich a mixture, a miscalculation in flight planning. As the end of the flight nears, the proximity of the destination becomes as tantalizing as the gauges' approach to empty is ominous. The pilot is transfixed by indecision. He knows he is perilously low on fuel. But gauges are crude and approximate, "unusable" fuel is really usable in level coordinated flight, probably the manufacturer built in a little safety margin, and besides, he has always been a lucky person.

The pilot started nibbling on his legal reserve somewhere south of Tallahassee. There were still a couple of airports along Florida's west coast at which he could have landed to refuel from self-service pumps. For that matter, if, 100 miles short of PIE, he had throttled back and leaned the mixture, he could have made the airport. Arriving in darkness with a quart or two of fuel remaining would not have been something to be proud of, but it would have been better than what actually happened.

The National Transportation Safety Board took its time with this accident, issuing its determination of probable cause 19 months later — six months to a year is more typical. The finding was sufficiently sensational for local newspapers to return to the cold case with fresh headlines. The cause, the Board wrote, was "the pilot's inadequate fuel planning, which resulted in a total loss of engine power due to fuel exhaustion."

"Contributing to the accident," it went on, "was the pilot's impairment due to cocaine use."

The toxicology report included evidence not only of cocaine use implicitly judged to have been within the time span of the trip, but of earlier use of crack cocaine — a cheaper, solid version of the drug that is smoked rather than inhaled or injected — and of cocaine in tandem with alcohol. The drug "likely affected [the pilot's] fuel planning abilities and en route fuel management."

Cocaine is a stimulant that people use because it makes them feel powerful, alert, focused and confident and produces, for an hour or two, a sense of excited euphoria. These agreeable effects are followed by physical discomfort, nervousness, fatigue coupled with insomnia, and a renewed craving for the drug, which is highly addictive.

The NTSB provides a laundry list of "additional effects ... expected ... with chronic ingestion", including "inability to focus on divided attention tasks, inability to follow directions, confusion [and] time distortion." From this description you would suppose that any habitual cocaine user would be an incompetent wreck, but in fact in some fields, notably entertainment, cocaine use is common and the drug's stimulant effects are apparently found to be more helpful, at least in the short term, than damaging.

Although the NTSB report implies that the pilot's use of cocaine may have been habitual, it seems possible that if he ingested it before or during this trip it was simply in order to help him remain alert during the long hours of night flying. If so, he may not have reckoned with an unintended side effect: the feeling of empowerment and self-confidence that the drug creates. There is much to deter a pilot from making an inconvenient en route stop when he is practically at his destination. The decision to do so must arise from reason and cool analysis, not from emotion. The "impairment" to which the NTSB referred may have taken the form of a euphoria — that adolescent feeling that nothing can go wrong — just sufficient to overcome the pilot's rational caution.

In the Black

On a November night in 1995, a Beech Baron 58 departed from Runway 24 at Cleveland's Burke Lakefront Airport (BKL), on the south shore of Lake Erie. It was bound for Raleigh, NC, with five aboard. The Baron climbed to 200 feet above the end of the runway and began a right turn. The tower controller, who had been watching the airplane, turned away. A couple of minutes later, a call came from a city operations office asking whether he could see smoke out on the lake.

The Baron had hit the water about six miles from the airport. The Coast Guard rescued two surviving passengers; the 1,000-hour instrument-rated pilot, 47, and two other passengers perished. The surviving passengers recalled no problem with the airplane or the pilot prior to impact.

A Gulfstream pilot, who took off shortly after the Baron, related to National Transportation Safety Board investigators that there was no visible horizon over the lake, and he would become disoriented if he took his eyes off his instruments to look out. The NTSB's report faulted the Baron's pilot for his failure to maintain a positive rate of climb after takeoff. It made no mention of spatial disorientation, but did cite the lack of visual references over the water as a factor.

On a clear, moonlit evening in January, 2008, another Baron 58 left BKL for Niagara Falls. The pilot, 68, an 18,000-hour ATP and CFII with a stack of ratings, was alone. He took off from Runway 24 with instructions to turn right on course. The tower controller watched as the Baron climbed, banked to the right, and then descended in a steepening arc and plunged into the lake. A fire burned briefly on the water.

The airplane and the remains of the pilot were recovered. Neither the engines themselves not the onboard engine monitor gave any indication of trouble; both engines were developing high power until the recording stopped. The flight control system appeared to have been intact up to impact.

Although the pilot had reported using only a cholesterol-regulating drug with no side effects relevant to flying, post mortem toxicology found two pain-killers and a heart-disease-related drug in his blood and urine. The pilot's personal medical records revealed that he suffered from mild diabetes, back pain, hypertension, gastric reflux and various cardiac problems. The NTSB did not say that any of these conditions or medications had had anything to do with his flying into the lake; but it seemed to suggest, by enumerating them, that they could have.

This time, the NTSB did not fault the pilot for "improper IFR procedure," as it had in the previous accident. Instead, it said he had become spatially disoriented as he turned out over the dark lake and away from the moon and the lights of Cleveland. Among the positional illusions that occur in the absence of visual references the NTSB cited the "somatogravic illusion," the impression of leaning backward — and therefore of being in a climbing attitude — that is produced when forward acceleration presses you against your seat back.

The available evidence in the two accidents was essentially identical. Shifting the blame from the pilot's actions to an external cause — spatial disorientation — may reflect a cultural shift at the NTSB, but changes nothing about the events.

In December, 2016, an hour before midnight, a Cessna Citation CJ4 took off from Runway 24 at BKL with instructions to turn right to 330 and maintain 2,000 feet.

You know what happened next.

The pilot, in this case, was 45 years old and had 1,200 hours. He had acquired his CJ4 single-pilot type rating just three weeks before the accident, but had previously owned a Cessna 510 Mustang for two years and logged 370 hours in it. As is customary in single-pilot jet operations, the pilot had been trained to engage the autopilot shortly after takeoff.

The NTSB's theory of the accident was that the pilot believed he had engaged the autopilot, but, for whatever reason, it had failed to engage. Slight differences between the panels of the CJ4 and his previous jet led to "mode confusion" and the pilot's failing to notice that the autopilot annunciator in the PFD was not illuminated.

The common thread among these three accidents was a takeoff in darkness followed by a climbing turn toward the "black hole" of the lake. Any turn requires some back pressure on the yoke; otherwise the nose will drop. In visual conditions, the need to maintain a climbing attitude is obvious to the pilot. Lacking visual cues, the pilot must obey the instruments. A distracted pilot may rely on a physical sensation of climbing that can exist even when the airplane is descending.

In the 1995 accident, the five occupants of the Baron had delayed their departure an hour in the vain hope of glimpsing a popular singer who was to be a passenger on the Gulfstream. Perhaps the group was convivial; the cockpit may not have been quite "sterile." The pilot evidently failed to monitor his instruments; the airplane flew into the water in a sufficiently shallow descent to allow two passengers to survive.

The 2008 crash was a little different. The pilot was not distracted by passengers, but he may have been fatigued, drowsy, affected by medication or otherwise compromised. The NTSB noted in passing that he had failed to remove the chocks during his preflight, and after starting the engines "jumped" the chocks to begin taxiing.

The Citation accident, however, is harder to explain. Unlike the Baron, the jet had an enhanced ground proximity warning system (EGPWS) as well as flight data and cockpit voice recorders. Apart from an unremarkable error in the pilot's readback of the departure control frequency, everything on the CVR is normal as the takeoff begins. The pilot remarks, "That's when it's nice to have more thrust than you need." The sound of movement of the landing gear handle is heard at 22:56:49.3; the jet is soon climbing at 6,000 fpm.

The following is the remainder of the CVR transcript. Automated voices, including altitude and EGPWS warnings, are in italics.

22:57:09.4	*Altitude.*
22:57:23.4	*Altitude.*
22:57:25.3	[Sound of engine power decrease]
22:57:27.2	*Bank angle. Bank angle.*
22:57:28.6	614SB contact departure. Safe flight.
22:57:30.8	To departure, 614SB.

At this point the pilot had begun to correct his bank angle, which had briefly exceeded 60 degrees, and to regain his assigned altitude, which he had overshot by nearly 900 feet. Evidently he was still hand flying the airplane.

22:57:37.1	614SB, Lake[front tower, you on]
22:57:39.1	*Sink rate. Sink rate.*
22:57:39.7	614SB.
22:57:41.4	[Sound of increasing air noise]
22:57:43.6	*Pull up.*
22:57:45.2	*Pull up.*
22:57:46.2	[Sound of overspeed warning begins and continues to end]
22:57:46.8	*Pull up.*
22:57:48.4	*Pull up.*
22:57:50.0	*Pull up.*
22:57:51.6	*Pull up.*
22:57:53.1	*Pull up.*
22:57:53.8	[Recording ends]

There was no evidence of a mechanical malfunction or catastrophic event such as a bird strike. The condition of the recovered remains of the pilot precluded an autopsy or toxicology. The recorded trajectory of the airplane was analyzed by computer simulation, with the conclusion that "the flight path was consistent with the performance of the airplane and no loss of control was evident from the data."

The NTSB's finding of probable cause was spatial disorientation, to which fatigue — the pilot had been awake for 17 hours — "mode confusion" over the status of the autopilot and "negative learning transfer" from the familiar Mustang to the new Citation all contributed.

You would suppose that even a single "pull up" warning should send your eyes straight to the attitude instruments. Evidently, however, the subjective sensations of spatial disorientation can be so persuasive that for 14 warning-crammed seconds an experienced jet pilot could think his instruments were peddling fake news.

More Than He Could Chew

Late in August of 2015, a 55-year-old Pennsylvania lawyer bought a 1981 A36 Bonanza. A private pilot with an instrument rating and around 800 hours of flight time, he had, according to a friend, "a lot" of IFR experience in a fixed-gear, fixed-pitch Piper Cherokee. The Bonanza, however, equipped with a Garmin 530 EFIS and a flight director, was more airplane than he was used to.

He quickly obtained a "complex" checkout — 6 hours in flight and an hour and a half of ground instruction — from an instructor whom he knew. The instructor showed him how to set the Garmin up for IFR approaches, but the approaches they flew together were in VMC, without a hood. The instructor cautioned the pilot not to fly in actual IFR conditions until he had more experience with the airplane and its equipment.

A few days later, the pilot, accompanied by his wife, her father, and a friend who owned a similarly equipped A36, flew to Florida to visit a daughter. The friend remained in Florida; on September 7, the others began the return trip northward.

Just before the leg from Sarasota to Greensboro, NC, the pilot filed an IFR flight plan — 190 knots at 8,000 feet must have been a gratifying change for someone used to a PA-28 — and got a telephone weather briefing. He cut the briefing short because thunderstorms were approaching from the west and he wanted to get away before they arrived. The just-under-four-hour flight, in VMC, from Sarasota to Greensboro was uneventful. At the destination airport, Piedmont Triad (GSO), however, he found an 1,100-foot overcast. The cloud layer was 1,500 feet deep.

The pilot asked the approach controller whether he should expect a visual approach. The question implies that he had seen breaks in the overcast, but the controller told him to expect the ILS to Runway 5R, and he did not demur.

Presumably the pilot attempted to set up the Garmin for the approach, as he had practiced; but he must quickly have become mired in confusion. The 530 is intimidating to a novice, with 20 knobs and buttons on its face and a near-infinity of menu choices. The pilot's distraction was such that he had to be told three times that his runway was 5R, not 5L.

The approach controller assigned a heading of 020 to intercept the localizer. The Bonanza was then 9 miles from the initial approach fix, PAGAN intersection. About two minutes later, the pilot asked the controller, "How do you like this route of flight?" The controller took the unconventional question in stride, replying that the airplane seemed to be a little to the right of course; he amended the heading to 360, a 20-degree adjustment. Surprisingly, the pilot asked, "Turning left or turning right for 360?" Non-standard phraseology and illogical questions are often early signs that a pilot is headed for trouble.

A little later, the controller asked, "Are you established on the localizer?"

"I believe I am," the pilot said.

But the Bonanza had flown through the localizer again. The pilot requested "vectors to final" — by which he possibly intended something like the virtually obsolete GCA, in which the controller guides the plane all the way to the runway. Instead, the controller canceled the ILS clearance and vectored the Bonanza back around for another try. While the controller was talking to another facility on a land line, the Bonanza pilot called again asking for vectors. His voice was "strained," and the controller noticed that he was at 2,500 feet rather than the assigned 3,000.

124

Finally, the pilot said, "We need a descent, we are almost disoriented."

The controller now realized that the pilot was in trouble. He decided to simplify matters by giving him no-gyro turns rather than vectors. He had his radar screen set at so wide a view, however, that he did not discern that the pilot was actually flying in circles, first to the right, then to the left. The Bonanza continued to lose altitude.

Finally, the controller told the pilot to climb and maintain 4,000 feet, above the overcast. "I'll block altitude for you." He thought that once in the sunshine above the clouds the pilot would be able to collect and re-orient himself.

But the Bonanza did not climb. It continued to descend, whether deliberately or inadvertently. Fortunately, the terrain below was relatively flat, and the airplane emerged from the clouds in one piece. But that was not to be the end of the story. Witnesses on the ground saw the airplane maneuvering erratically and banking steeply. It "looked as if it were a trick plane practicing stunts, or else someone trying to stabilize the plane but continuing to overcorrect..." Surprisingly, although he was now in good VFR conditions below the overcast, the pilot, desperate to locate the runway, never regained control. Perhaps panic, or vertigo, had become too extreme for him to claw his way back. The A36 stalled and spun before crashing 7 miles from GSO, almost exactly beneath the Runway 5L ILS. No one survived.

The NTSB's finding of probable cause exposes the difficulty the Board sometimes has with the concept of "cause." The cause of the accident, the Board says, was spatial disorientation. Certainly, that is true. But the pilot's in-flight decision-making, which put him in the position of having to make an ILS approach, against the advice of his instructor, with still-unfamiliar equipment, is not mentioned, even though the narrative strongly suggests that the pilot became disoriented at least partly because he was overwhelmed by his new equipment.

The Board criticized the FAA for failing to train controllers "to recognize and effectively respond to disorientation scenarios." The Board objected that no-gyro turns in both directions may have worsened the pilot's disorientation, and was scandalized that most controllers at the facility were unfamiliar with the concept of a standard rate turn. The exact rate at which a pilot turns during a no-gyro approach is, however, of little importance to a controller.

Something to notice about this accident is how the pilot's ability to cope deteriorates over time, to the point that he can no longer even avail himself of the seemingly elementary expedient of climbing back above the clouds in a straight line.

It is important for pilots, and particularly low-time pilots, to understand that the very stress of trying to solve a problem may erode one's power to solve it. Unlike most other challenges in our lives, those encountered in airplanes may be life-threatening. In menacing circumstances, the brain seems to become blinkered, abandoning rational analysis in favor of raw impulse or, worse, total paralysis. You may overlook the obvious and make unreasonable choices. You may find yourself unable to interpret the readings on your instruments. You will not perform as well as you expect, and certainly not so well as you did in the same situation on a check ride or in a simulator. That is why it is so important not to skirt risk closely, but to give it a wide berth.

First There Is a Mountain

The 77-year-old, 8,000-hour pilot-owner of a Cessna 182, accompanied by his wife, flew from Anchorage to Juneau, Alaska on a July afternoon. The couple had been in the process of moving to Hoonah, about 31 nm west-southwest of Juneau; the ostensible purpose of this trip was to position the 182 there before the start of winter. The pilot's wife intended to return to Anchorage; but the 505-nm IFR trip took longer than expected, and her Alaska Airlines flight was taxiing out when they arrived. She rebooked for the following morning, and the couple then flew over to Hoonah for the night.

Her flight back to Anchorage was to depart at 7:28 a.m. At 6:43, the local controller at Juneau received a call from the pilot, reporting 10 miles southwest for landing. The controller told him to report four miles out. A moment later, a faint ELT signal was picked up in the tower and also at the Juneau Flight Service Station.

Delayed by worsening weather, searchers located the wreckage of the 182 the next day in mountainous terrain a few miles south of the Juneau airport. The airplane had struck the descending side of a ridge on Douglas Island, coming to rest on a rock ledge at the 3,100-foot level. The impact had been sufficiently violent that the engine, propeller and nosewheel had broken away from the airframe and tumbled 900 feet down into the valley below.

Juneau lies amid a jumble of islands, inlets, channels, fjords and peaks. The climate tends toward the cloudy and wet; Ketchikan, a little farther south, enjoys between 12 and 13 feet of rain a year. On the day of the accident, however, the weather was not bad: Hoonah was reporting 10 miles visibility under a 3,500-foot overcast, with calm winds; Juneau five miles, 2,800 broken, 3,600 overcast. The mountains south of Juneau, however, were misty and obscured.

Douglas Island lies directly south of Juneau. The peaks in its center rise to 3,350 feet. A straight line from Hoonah to Juneau International Airport (KJNU) just misses northern shore of Douglas Island, but crosses a 1,200-foot ridge on the Mansfield Peninsula, halfway between Hoonah and Juneau.

The pilot carried two handheld Garmin GPS units, a 195 and a 495. Neither was badly damaged in the crash, and accident investigators were able to download position and altitude logs for the fatal trip from both.

The ground track was not perfectly straight, but it was straight enough to suggest an airplane being hand flown along a GPS course. Curiously, the course was not that from Hoonah to the Juneau airport; instead, it pointed toward Juneau Harbor Seaplane Base (5Z1), six miles southeast of International. One of the GPS units contained a previously stored program for a flight from Hoonah to the seaplane base; it seemed probable that the pilot had somehow selected it by mistake.

Six miles is a small difference, but when the total distance to be flown is only 31 miles the angular error is 13 degrees, and in the mountainous terrain surrounding Juneau it had the effect of putting obstacles in the pilot's way that ought not to have been there. The first was a 3,300-foot peak on the Mansfield Peninsula. The preceding evening that ridge had been several miles to his left as he flew from Juneau to Hoonah; now, strangely, it was right in his way, and he had to swerve, and climb 600 feet, to avoid it.

Nine miles farther along, he should have had Juneau in sight; his groundspeed was 125 knots and he had been airborne for 15 minutes. He had already called to report that he was 10 miles southwest — a figure that actually reflected the GPS-reported distance from the seaplane base. But now he encountered another oddity: a second ridge where there should have been none at all.

He may have been flying in mist just below the overcast, or between layers. The illumination was fair; the Alaskan summer sun had been up for two hours. He was level at 2,800 feet, but then started to climb. To judge from the altitudes in the GPS log, which were recorded ten times per minute, he must have been surprised by the steepness of the ridge, because, after several seconds of climbing gradually at 89 knots groundspeed, the 182 suddenly shot upward from 3,166 feet to 3,583 feet at 2,000 fpm, while its groundspeed dropped to 34 knots.

It cleared the ridge, but crashed a short distance past it. Perhaps it had stalled; five seconds after the 34-knot point, one more entry was made in the GPS log, with a groundspeed of 41 knots.

As the NTSB explained it:

Given the lack of mechanical deficiencies with the airplane, the absence of any distress communications, and the pilot's self-induced pressure to get his wife to the airport to avoid missing her flight, it is likely the pilot flew into instrument meteorological conditions while tracking his portable GPS receiver to the wrong destination and subsequently collided with mountainous terrain.

This accident encourages reflection upon the nature of mistakes. Everyone makes them. Probably some people are more aware of their mistakes than others are. There have been accidents caused by careless data entry, improper altimeter setting, radio frequencies off by one digit. If it can be done wrong, someone will. Of course, far more mistakes are made than lead to accidents; the vast majority are inconsequential, and so we regard them, and our propensity for them, with indulgence.

Our pilot had flown from Juneau to Hoonah just the previous evening, and must have made the trip many times before, and so the general lay of the land was known to him. Why was it necessary at all to use GPS to go 30 miles in a straight line among a host of unambiguous landmarks? But he did; perhaps it seemed convenient, or to provide an extra layer of assurance, or simply to be fun.

One defense again navigational mistakes goes by the name of "situational awareness." Unfortunately, you can be highly aware of your situation, completely tuned in to the task of flying, and yet be operating in some mistaken conception about what that situation actually is. Our pilot probably believed that he had everything under control; after all, he had not one but two GPSs, and they agreed with one another.

Something built into our brains inclines us to ignore evidence that conflicts with expectation. In this case, the pilot, having selected, as he believed, the Hoonah-to-

Juneau route on his GPS units, had a strong, and
reasonable, expectation that as long as they showed him
to be on that track, he must be in the right place.

Now, cruising at 3,000 feet, he encountered a mountain.
He climbed and made a sudden deviation to the left to
avoid it. Where had that mountain been when he made
the same trip, in the opposite direction, yesterday
evening?

Perhaps he said to himself that last evening he must have
been slightly north of the straight-line course, and so this
peak had been a few miles off to his left. A glance at the
GPS screens would reassure him: there was the course
line, there was the mountain. From this point to Juneau, it
should all be open water.

Then a second mountain loomed. This was more of a
problem. The first mountain could be explained as a
slight track error. This one should not exist at all. Things
began happening rapidly — too rapidly to allow the pilot
to analyze them. The ground was coming up in front of
him. It was already too late.

Today, situational awareness is increasingly being
transferred from pilots' brains to their microchips. There
is no straightforward protection, other than double- and
triple-checking every action, against the type of clerical
errors that we may make in our interactions with digital
devices. Two GPS units provide no redundancy if both
are confirming you in the same mistake. What is needed

— and remains available, at least when the terrain is visible and while we still have the VOR network at our disposal — is independent confirmation that we are where we think we are. Visual navigation ought to be a constant cycle of expectation and confirmation: Charts and terrain should come together like two sides of a zipper.

You remember — it's what we used to call "pilotage."

The Only One to Fly

On a Thursday in March, 2013, the 500-hour pilot of a
Mooney M20E arrived at Angel Fire, a ski resort east of
Taos in the Sangre de Cristo Mountains of New Mexico.
With him were his girlfriend, his sister and his sister's
13-year-old daughter. They came from San Antonio,
stayed with a cousin of the pilot, and planned to return on
Sunday.

At midday on Sunday they were at the airport. The wind
was blowing — *really* blowing, 33 knots gusting to 47 —
right across the runway. There were standing lenticulars
on the mountaintops and the forecast bristled with
warnings of possible rotors. The lifts on the ski slopes
had shut down. The runway, in a bowl surrounded by
mountain ridges, was known to be subject to
unpredictable turbulence. Nobody was flying.

An employee of the FBO, an A&P mechanic with long experience in aviation, tried to suggest to the pilot that the conditions were not ideal. "You're really going to fly in this weather?" he asked, with, I suppose, barely disguised incredulity.

The pilot replied that he was, and it wasn't going to be a problem.

"My neighbor has a Mooney, and he waves off at 20 knots," the employee remarked, and went on to suggest that if the pilot cared to wait the wind might die down a bit toward sunset. The pilot, however, assured him that "his plane could handle it."

The employee's view of the subsequent takeoff roll was blocked by snow banks, but he caught sight of the Mooney when it was airborne. It seemed barely under control. Crabbing strongly to the west, seemingly unable to gain altitude, the airplane was being tossed like a cork in white water. "The right wing rose rapidly," he said, "the aircraft rotated left and the nose rose rapidly, the aircraft continued to rotate to the left until the nose pointed straight down toward the ground and then [it] flew vertically into the ground."

The reason for this accident was plain enough: "The pilot's loss of control while flying in a turbulent mountain-wave environment," the National Transportation Safety Board said. His overconfidence and inexperience were contributing factors.

This is an instance, it seems to me, where it would have made sense for the NTSB to shift the "cause" of the accident backward a little in time, to the pilot's decision to take off in the first place. Assuming that he was not acting out of sheer unreflecting bullheadedness, we must suppose that he weighed the pros and cons. What were they?

He had never before flown into or out of an airport as high as Angel Fire, but he had flown in the mountains in Colorado and Wyoming. If he consulted his POH, he would have found that even at the current density altitude of 9,550 feet the M20E ought to get off the ground in less than a quarter of the 8,900-foot runway and climb at 700 or 800 feet a minute.

The airport manager took a less sanguine view of the Mooney's likely performance. He was present on Thursday when the airplane arrived, and he noticed the "size" of the occupants and the quantity of luggage, which consisted of six "medium-sized" bags. He suggested to the pilot that he not buy fuel there unless he really needed to, but instead stop to refuel en route. The pilot agreed at the time, but in fact put six gallons of fuel into one tank before departing, bringing the fuel aboard to 28 gallons, or about 170 pounds.

Although one member of the party was quite portly, the combined weight of all four was less than the 4 times 170 for which the plane was designed. When they boarded for the fatal flight, however, the pilot seems not to have concerned himself about the CG location. The largest passenger was in the back seat and the smallest in the right front. The NTSB, doing a retrospective weight and balance, assigned an implausible weight of only 10 pounds to each of the six bags, but still found the CG to be slightly behind the aft limit. If, as seems certain, the bags were heavier than that, the airplane might have remained below its gross weight of 2,575 pounds but would have been still father out of CG limits and consequently less stable and harder to handle — not that, given the magnitude of the turbulence, additional longitudinal stability would have made a significant difference.

Viewed solely in terms of weight and takeoff performance, the decision to fly was defensible. Besides, from a certain point of view the terrain was favorable. They had only to follow the high tension lines to the southeast; the elevation in that direction barely exceeded 10,000 feet before falling rapidly toward the high plains. The Mooney should have no trouble gaining that much altitude, and the west wind would even help carry it upslope.

Furthermore, it was Sunday, and all four of the people in the plane probably had places they needed to be on Monday morning. Apart from the wind the weather was good, and they would enjoy a phenomenal tailwind on the way back to San Antonio.

The pilot and his sister talked to their father on the morning of the flight and told him that "it appeared to be a good day to fly." Whether this was a sincere judgment, an attempt to reassure the other passengers who might have been within earshot, or sheer whistling in the dark, we cannot know. The cousin with whom they were staying did not share the opinion and tried in vain to dissuade them from going. The 13-year-old expressed misgivings; none of the others did.

It's pretty certain that the pilot had never before taken off in a direct crosswind of 33 knots gusting to 47. Few pilots have. The M20 POH gives a maximum demonstrated crosswind velocity of 11 knots, so he was deep in terra incognita.

Even assuming that he knew to lean the mixture for maximum power before starting the takeoff roll, the airplane, with less than 150 horsepower available, would have accelerated slowly and would likely have begun to slide sideways before it was ready to fly. To avoid hitting the edge lights, he would probably have lifted it into the air sooner than he would have liked.

Now he would have confronted the siege of troubles that, being inexperienced in mountain flying, he could not have anticipated. Normally, you would accelerate to a higher-than-normal liftoff speed to provide a margin for gusts. But in an extremely strong direct crosswind it's very difficult, if not impossible, to keep the airplane tracking the centerline, and the only option, apart from aborting the takeoff, is to get airborne.

Off the ground at a low speed, the airplane would barely accelerate. At the same time, it was being tossed about by the wind. An 800-fpm rate of climb is not of much use in 1,000-fpm up- and downdrafts. Although he was in the air for more than a mile before crashing beyond the end of the runway, he never retracted the landing gear. It was probably all he could do to maintain even temporary and incomplete control.

The day after the accident, a reporter interviewed the airport manager, who had not been present at the airport when the crash occurred. "We sit in a bowl," he told her. "When the wind comes over the west ridge, it accelerates and tumbles and is hard for even experienced pilots to navigate." Asked why the airport had been open in spite of the wind, he explained that he only closed it for removing snow. "We assume that these pilots are smart enough to realize that they're not God. They can't do everything; the plane's only designed to do so much."

"You couldn't have paid me enough money to get in a plane yesterday," he said.

Point of No Return

On January 9, 2007, the pilot of a Cessna 207 prepared for a cargo flight from Kenai, Alaska, south of Anchorage, to Kokhanok, 125 miles to the southwest. It was around ten in the morning — but the winter sun was still below the horizon — when he started the engine, which had been warmed during the night by an electric heater. He taxied out, then immediately returned to the ramp, where he called his employer to report that the oil pressure, while still in the green, was lower than he expected it to be. The two discussed possible reasons for the unusual indication, including the low ambient temperature (though cold usually makes oil pressure rise, not drop). The pilot decided to continue with the flight, and said that he would monitor the oil pressure before crossing the Cook Inlet.

The sun was above the horizon when the pilot called the tower again for permission to taxi. Three minutes later he was in the air, and he reported to the company office that the oil pressure was "up in the green and good to go."

Kenai is located on the eastern shore of the Cook Inlet, an arm of water that is on average 20 miles wide. A little north of Kenai, however, the inlet narrows to less than nine miles. Perhaps because he was now running a little late, the pilot, who usually crossed the water at the narrowest point, reported that this morning he was going to "go down" from his normal route, meaning, apparently, that he was going to head a little to the south of it.

Less than ten minutes later, the pilot contacted Kenai tower. "I have a mayday. I've, ah, substantial vibration has occurred, ah, I can't see, ah, problem, I'm mid-channel, descending."

The Kenai tower controller asked for his position. "I'm mid-channel, headed for the (unintelligible) … I'm headed into the water." He gave his precise coordinates: 60:40.940 north latitude, 151:43.542 west longitude. "Mayday, mayday," he repeated, and nothing more.

The company's director of operations, preparing to take off himself in another plane, heard the mayday call and flew toward the area of the accident, as did several other aircraft. Despite the pilot's having given precise coordinates, there was some confusion about his location, and it was not until two hours later that an ELT signal was received and a ship located the airplane, which by then had been carried almost nine miles southwestward by the ebbing tide. Almost intact, the 207 was nose down in the water beside a foot-thick, 100-yard-long slab of floating ice on which a crewman reported seeing tire tracks leading to the point where the plane had gone over the edge.

The ship hoisted the airplane aboard. The pilot was not in it, and searchers were never able to locate his body. Time of survival in the freezing water would have been 30 minutes, of consciousness half that; the pilot was presumed to have survived the landing, but died in the water.

The 207's engine was destroyed, the crankcase punctured by the connecting rod of the #1 cylinder. Other rod bearings were scored and discolored by heat, and the oil screen was full of metal chips.

A portable GPS was removed from the wreckage and its record of the flight downloaded. The altitude at which the engine failure occurred was 1,439 feet. The stored ground track showed the airplane beginning to lose height and drifting somewhat southward before turning northwestward toward the promontory that projects from the western shore of the channel. At the time the pilot reported his latitude and longitude, he was 1.8 miles from shore and 100 feet above the water.

According to the owner's manual, the 207 would glide about 2.1 miles from an altitude of 1,500 feet, a ratio of 7.4:1. (Incidentally, the prop control was found in the cruise position. The pitch of a windmilling propeller significantly influences gliding performance, and the best glide requires coarse pitch, that is, low rpm and the prop

controller pulled all the way back.) The airplane would
have had to be at at least 3,500 feet at the middle of the
narrowest point of the channel to glide to either shore.
Where the water is 20 miles wide, a height of 7,000 feet
would be required just to reach shore.

The company's operations manual did not specifically
address the question of the altitude at which to fly over
water, but that, the owner explained, was because pilots
were expected to comply with the FAR. The FAR
contains a couple of references to overwater flight by
landplanes. Part 135.183 states that "No person may
operate a land aircraft carrying passengers over water
unless ... at an altitude that allows it to reach land in the
case of engine failure." This commonsense rule did not
strictly apply to the accident flight, however, because it
carried cargo, not passengers. Another pertinent section
is Part 91.205, which deals with equipment requirements,
and specifies that "if the aircraft is operated for hire over
water, and beyond power-off gliding distance from shore,
approved flotation gear [must be] readily available to
each occupant..." The pilot, in this case, had no survival
gear or flotation device.

 The owner of the company, who was also the chief pilot,
told the National Transportation Safety Board that he
usually crossed the Cook Inlet at its narrowest point,
which required flying a short distance northwest from the
base on Kenai. With regard to company policy, he said
that it was "to fly at an altitude that would allow an
airplane to reach shore ... The FAR requirement to

144

maintain adequate altitude over water to reach power-off gliding distance to shore, in the event personal flotation devices are not carried aboard the aircraft, is very clear, and this FAR is clearly covered in our training as well as the practical aspects of the requirement to maintain adequate altitude over water in a single-engine aircraft to reach a suitable landing area due to the very limited chance of survival in the event an aircraft does go down in the cold waters of Alaska."

The pilot had been hired about eight months earlier. He had over 5,000 hours at the time of the accident, including more than 500 hours in the Cessna 207. About four weeks after being hired, he had taken a Part 135 proficiency check with an FAA inspector at Anchorage, and had been found unsatisfactory in emergency procedures and judgment. He had passed on a retest the following day.

The NTSB finding of probable cause was: "The total loss of engine power during cruise flight ... which resulted in a ditching into ice covered ocean water. Factors contributing to the survivability of the accident were the pilot's improper decision to fly over frigid water without sufficient altitude to reach a suitable landing area, the lack of written policy and procedures by the operator requiring sufficient altitude to reach shore when crossing ocean waters, temperature extremes consisting of sub-zero air and below freezing water temperatures, and the lack of personal flotation/survival equipment."

The question of the lack of survival equipment is somewhat mooted by the fact that potential rescuers did not reach the airplane until after it had been in the water for over two hours, far beyond any expectation of human survival. There was no requirement to carry a raft, but even in a raft the pilot would have been exposed to -20 degree air temperatures for two hours while almost certainly soaking wet.

The issue of judgment is more pertinent. The pilot had been concerned enough about the low oil pressure to taxi back to the ramp and report it to his employer. Yet he seems to have allowed their discussion to lull him into a state of such complacency that, after stating that he would monitor the oil pressure after taking off, he neglected the elementary precaution, which a healthy respect for the Fates and Furies would commend even in temperate weather, of remaining within gliding distance of land. To be sure, a wise pilot would always remain within gliding distance of some landable place, whether flying over water or mountains or forests. But how many do?

A Novice in Icing

In the wake of the John Kennedy Jr. accident, various pundits who should have known better pontificated, without a shred of evidence, upon its cause and what ought to be done about it. You could see the mythmaking impulse at work. People seemed to want to believe that Kennedy was a spoiled, reckless fellow, and that the gods had swatted him down for his hubris. In support of this schema, press accounts, no doubt to the amazement and delight of the manufacturer's marketing department, transformed the plodding Piper Saratoga, the airborne equivalent of a Buick family sedan, into a "hot rod" that required a "butterfly touch" to fly. The possibility that Kennedy was actually cruising along cautiously on autopilot and had an electrical glitch that he didn't detect until too late was never even mentioned.

A great deal of rubbish was printed and broadcast.
Presumably most of it went into one of the public's
collective ears and out the other; but one notion that
seemed to stick was that if only Kennedy had had an
instrument rating, everything would have been all right.

An instrument rating is a seemingly simple preventive
for weather-related — or, in the Kennedy case, perhaps
visibility-related — accidents. For a long time the
aviation media exhorted pilots to get their instrument
ratings (an enterprise that fortuitously also helps sell
airplanes and equipment). The FAA joined in by
reducing and finally eliminating the flight experience
requirement for the rating. But the instrument rating is
two-edged. Perhaps it prevents a good many "continued
VFR" accidents; but another class that could be called
"amateur IFR" accidents took their place.

A case in point is the crash of a Piper Archer on a flight
from Chicago to Athens, Ohio. The male pilot was killed
and the woman passenger was seriously injured. The
accident scenario illustrates the pitfalls of combining an
instrument rating with general inexperience.

A front lay over Columbus, Ohio. The pair had already
delayed the flight a day because of weather. It was now
Tuesday; the woman needed to get to Athens for a class
on Wednesday. The pilot called the Kankakee Flight
Service Station at 6:45 a.m. and received reports of rime
or mixed icing in Ohio between 2,000 and 13,000 feet.
"Pretty tough conditions for a PA-28," the briefer

remarked. After noting that the pilot would have good alternates if he couldn't get into Athens, the briefer added, "My main concern on this…one is gonna be ice."

"Yeah," the pilot replied, "but it sounds like once I get out of Chicago…the only pilot report you got on that is higher up."

The briefer, not persuaded that the absence of pilot reports proved the absence of ice, returned, "I've got… temperatures for that entire route ranging from minus six to minus eight degrees [Celsius]…I don't have any top reports either, that's the problem." The temperature range was that in which icing might occur, and the lack of tops reports meant that the pilot could not be sure of climbing above the weather.

Still, surface conditions around Columbus were not bad: 1,000 to 1,500-foot ceilings, visibilities of two to three miles in light rain and fog. The winds aloft were very favorable: out of the northwest at over 30 knots.

After a fifteen-minute briefing the pilot filed an IFR flight plan.

According to the passenger, it was very foggy and cold when they took off from Meigs Field in Chicago. But the flight was apparently uneventful until 1016:33 CST, when the pilot radioed to the north radar controller at Columbus Approach Control that he was losing engine power. He was then at 9,000 feet, near the Appleton

VOR, between Columbus and Mount Vernon, Ohio. "What can I do for you now?" said the controller. "Vectors to the nearest airport," replied the pilot, and added that the engine was still developing "a little bit of power." The controller supplied vectors to the Knox County Airport at Mount Vernon, 12.5 miles away to the northeast. At 1017:30 the controller cleared the pilot to "...descend and maintain 3,000 that is at pilot's discretion on the altitude." A few seconds later the controller gave the pilot the weather for Port Columbus, and said, "You're presently 13 miles northeast of Port Columbus if you want to try there." The pilot replied that he would take Port Columbus.

What happened next is not clear from the National Transportation Safety Board's report on the accident, but the pilot presumably turned toward Port Columbus, a heading of about 220 degrees and slightly upwind. When he asked, about a minute later, how far it was now to Port Columbus, the controller told him he was 15 miles from the airport. Shortly thereafter, the pilot received a frequency change to the final radar controller for Port Columbus. At this point, the Archer's altitude was between 3,800 and 4,000 feet.

At 1020:27, almost three minutes after the earlier controller had told the pilot that he was 13 miles from Port Columbus, the final controller told him the same thing. The controller asked the pilot if he was using carburetor heat; "Yeah, I did," he replied, "it's not working." He then asked, "Anything closer than Port

150

Columbus?" At 1021:03 the controller told him that
Knox County airport was northeast, and gave him a
heading of 040 — opposite to the direction he had been
flying up to now. At 1021:21, the final controller revised
the heading to 130 degrees without, apparently,
explaining to the bewildered pilot that he was now
directing him to a third airport, Newark. When the pilot
asked the distance to the airport, the controller replied 11
miles.

More than five minutes had now passed since the pilot
had begun his descent. He must have felt that the airports
were deliberately avoiding him. After another three
minutes the final controller informed the pilot that he had
reports of light rime icing "all the way down to the final"
for Port Columbus. At 1025:54 the pilot asked, "…how
far from the airport and wind direction please." The
controller replied that he was six and a half miles
northwest. There were no further communications from
the airplane. It crashed in an open field near Granville,
Ohio, about five miles short of the Newark Heath airport.

On reaching the ground the airplane stopped rapidly —
the wreckage path was only 83 feet long — but remained
upright and substantially intact. The flaps were retracted.
The Granville fire chief arrived on the scene at about
1050, and observed scattered pieces of ice about half an
inch thick whose shape conformed to that of the leading
edges of the wings. Accident investigators examined the
airplane on the day of the accident and the following day.
They found no sign of mechanical failure, but noted that

the spark plugs were heavily sooted — an indication of excessively rich operation, which could be due to restriction of engine breathing by ice.

NTSB investigators interviewed the controllers more than three months after the accident, attempting to determine the reason for the puzzling series of vectors the pilot had received. The first controller said that he gave the pilot a vector to Knox County (at Mount Vernon) because it was the closest airport, he thought it would have VFR conditions, the terrain around it was flat, and the wind would be at the pilot's back. He provided Columbus weather because it was the closest official weather he had immediately available, though he could have gotten Knox County weather by telephone. He denied that he had "offered" the pilot Port Columbus, and said that he was puzzled by the pilot's decision to go to there, since the airport was IFR.

The final controller explained that he first gave the pilot a vector to Knox County because he believed it to be the nearest airport. But he then realized that Newark was slightly closer and more downwind, and so he issued a revised heading. (The airplane's earlier apparent failure to progress toward Port Columbus for several minutes remains unexplained.)

The Area Supervisor provided, among other things, the boilerplate statement that a controller's primary responsibility is to be responsive to a pilot's desires, and to direct the pilot to the nearest airport if he requests it.

As everyone knows, the ultimate responsibility for the safety of a flight rests with the pilot. Although the FSS briefer clearly felt that it was not advisable to fly a small airplane through the weather that existed that day, the pilot decided differently, and had a right to. He recognized the risk of icing and mentioned it to his passenger, but assured her that if they got into icing, they would be able to get out of it quickly. He flew at a high altitude, presumably because he expected that icing would be less likely at lower temperatures. (The tops, unbeknownst to him, were at 10,000; a little higher and he would have been out of the weather.)

The most likely explanation of the loss of engine power is induction system icing. The pilot's statement that he had tried carb heat and it hadn't worked suggests that he was not using carb heat continuously in cruise. If the problem was in the carburetor, then the power loss would compromise the engine's ability to generate enough heat to melt away the ice. If the icing obstructed the air supply to the engine ahead of the carburetor, on the other hand, carburetor heat could have no effect.

Once the emergency existed, the responsibility for the flight remained with the pilot. If he had been following the progress of the flight on his charts he would have known that he was roughly equidistant from three airports, but two lay roughly crosswind from him whereas one (Newark) lay downwind; this information could be deduced from either VFR or IFR charts. But few pilots fly with a fingernail upon their current position, and so it is reasonable for a pilot to ask controllers for information.

In this case, however, the pilot seems to have placed himself entirely in the controllers' hands. Although he descended for many minutes, there is no record of his discussing with them his exact position, or the options available, or of his asking them to obtain weather at all airports within gliding range. There is in fact no mention of gliding range at all, although for an airplane like the Archer one could expect to glide, in still air, about one and a half miles per thousand feet of altitude above the ground — in this case, about 12 miles. The matter was complicated by the fact that the Archer still had some power, and by the strong tailwind; but there was plenty of time for both pilot and controllers to figure out that Port Columbus and Knox were marginal, while because of the tailwind Newark was golden. The remaining engine power could not be counted on, in any case; the emergency descent had to be planned as if it were a dead stick glide.

It's natural for an inexperienced pilot — this pilot's total time was 232 hours — to defer to controllers, who seem like omniscient authority figures. The very name "controller" encourages this deference. In emergencies, however, controllers are reluctant to trespass on the pilot's authority, and seldom question pilots' decisions even when, as in this case, they seem to be bad ones. Controllers don't want to assume responsibility for life-

or-death situations which they have a limited power to affect. The pilot, like it or not, accepts all the risks and responsibilities when he decides to fly. In this case the pilot, who knew his groundspeed and the gliding ability of his airplane, could have reached Newark. But he first accepted the selection of Knox County, then seemingly seized on what was, at most, an implied endorsement of Port Columbus, even though Port Columbus was probably out of gliding range and slightly upwind. His indecisiveness in the emergency was in contrast with the boldness with which he decided to make the flight in the first place. Both can be attributed to inexperience, and to the enlarged menu of dangers that the instrument rating places before a novice pilot.

Incapacitation

At a dinner gathering, a few days after the wonderfully well-omened USAir ditching in the Hudson, when several guests had been grilling me about bird strikes and ditching procedures, someone commented that her worst nightmare was being in an airplane when the pilot had a heart attack.

"How often," another guest asked me, "does that happen?"

I had no idea, nor a smartphone from which to obtain an immediate answer. Later, however, I searched the NTSB accident database for all reports from the past ten years in which the word "cardiac" occurs. Forty-three appeared.

As with all such searches, there were some spurious results. For instance, a statement like "The autopsy disclosed no evidence of a cardiac abnormality" turns up alongside "The pilot was incapacitated by a cardiac event." Furthermore, in many instances an autopsy reveals various degrees of heart disease, and the investigator feels obliged to speculate that it could have had a role. Still, many of these accidents involve common scenarios, such as descending too low on an instrument approach or becoming disoriented after takeoff on a dark night — occasionally with the help of cannabis or Jack Daniels — and so there is no special need to suppose that a heart attack caused the accident.

In addition to those cases, there were a few, classified as incidents rather than accidents, in which death occurred after a safe landing or a non-fatal accident, and one in which the pilot of a seaplane experienced a "transient ischemic attack" or "mini-stroke," blacked out, crashed into a lake, and was rescued. In this category were, remarkably, two instances of fatal heart attacks occurring after the respective pilots had landed their helicopters on oil rigs in the Gulf of Mexico; to augment the improbability by a factor of 12, both occurred in the month of May, two years apart.

There remained 12 events in which a heart attack was the likely cause of a crash. In eight of these, the pilot was alone in the airplane.

In a few instances, pilots may have been unaware of their heart disease. This was the NTSB's judgment in the case of an 11,500-hour ATP whose Cessna T210 plunged into the Pacific Ocean off Dana Point, California, with four aboard, and also in that of the owner of a Smith Aerostar 600 that crashed, also in the Pacific, near Catalina Island, during a post-maintenance test flight. More often than not, however, the pilot knew he had a heart problem but chose to keep flying.

In one such case, 11 minutes after taking off from Palm Beach International the private pilot of a Mooney M20J reported to the departure controller that he was returning with a "severe, severe headache in the base of [his] neck." Two minutes later, he said, "My defibrillator just went off on me." Two minutes after this, the pilot said that he was losing his sight and turning eastward, toward the Atlantic, because "I don't wanna take anybody out [and] I don't know whether I can make it back." The Mooney flew out to sea for seven minutes before crashing into the water.

The pilot understood what was happening to him because he knew that he was suffering from serious cardiac disease. He had had a valve replacement and bypass surgery two years earlier, and had had a defibrillator implanted six months after that. He had experienced numerous instance of lightheadedness, defibrillator discharge, and abnormal heart rhythms, sometimes while flying. He had not tried to renew his medical certification, last issued four years earlier, presumably because he knew that his condition would disqualify him from flying.

In another case, a 29,000-hour retired airline pilot flew a Wittman Tailwind into the Pacific Ocean off the coast of Southern California. (The persistent appearance of oceans in these accounts is unexplained.) The pilot, whose personal medical records revealed a history of "hypercholesterolemia, hypertension, obesity, sleep apnea, gastroesophageal reflux disease, prostrate [sic] carcinoma, radiation colitis, a possible cerebrovascular accident, and mild dementia of Alzheimer's type," had agreed with the partner with whom he co-owned the airplane that he would not fly it by himself; but on that pleasant January morning he took off alone and flew to the Long Beach harbor, where witnesses observed the little homebuilt in a long, shallow, seemingly controlled descent — "it appeared that the airplane was landing in the water" — that ended in a collision with the ocean.

Like many pilots beset by dangerous medical conditions late in life, this one had concealed or minimized them on his medical application. So had a professional cropduster who crashed, killing himself and his wife, in a rented 172. In the wreckage investigators found a bag of prescription medicines which, his medical examiner later said, would have disqualified him from flying had the examiner known about them. He had, however, reported his use of two heart medicines, an anti-arrhythmic and an anti-anginal, and had been flying with restricted medical certification since having triple bypass surgery seven years earlier.

Not so the pilot of a Cherokee who, with his wife, crashed into a Southern California lake in 1998. He had had a heart attack twenty years earlier, and had repeatedly applied for medical certification and been denied. He had also repeatedly asserted on his applications that he had never been denied a medical. He had finally obtained a third-class medical in the year before the accident, but it was under review. At the time of the accident he was taking an over-the-counter medication that was contraindicated for people with heart disease because it irritated the heart. The NTSB report on the accident notes that the injuries of his wife, who was not a pilot, were "consistent with control manipulation at impact."

Non-reporting of disqualifying medical conditions rose to a crescendo in a non-instrument-rated pilot who took off, with a passenger, in dense fog, and promptly crashed. While the cause of the accident may have been disorientation rather than incapacitation, the list of the pilot's afflictions, obtained from his doctor by subpoena, is startling: "hypercholesterolemia, fibromyalgia, fatigue, sclerodactyly, scleroderma, gastroesophageal reflux, CREST syndrome, chronic neuropathy... secondary to previous back injury and surgeries and lumbar stenosis, chronic anxiety and depression, panic attacks, OSA (obstructive sleep apnea), BPH (benign prostatic hypertrophy). His documented medications between

160

1998 and 2002 include: Lipitor [atorvastatin], Flomax
[tamsulosin], Restoril [temazepam], Serzone
[nefazodone], Ultram [tramadol], Buspar [buspirone],
Prozac [fluoxetine], Wellbutrin [bupropion], Remeron
[mirtazapine], Pepcid [famotidine]."

"From 1998 to 2002, " the NTSB report continues, "the
pilot did not report any of these diagnoses on his FAA
airman medical certificate application nor did he report
his use of these medications except for the following:
Lipitor, Pepcid, Flomax."

While in several cases a pilot was aware of his heart
problems but concealed them from FAA medical
examiners, in one instance the examiner, a friend of the
pilot, appeared to have concealed from the FAA his
knowledge of the pilot's many disqualifying conditions
over a period of years. The 77-year-old pilot, who had
reported 16,500 hours total time and 500 hours in the
previous six months on his last medical application, had
a long history of heart attacks, surgery, and chronic heart
disease, all of which he denied, with the help of his
medical-examiner friend, on his medical applications. He
was alone, on a wildlife survey flight in northern
Michigan, when his 182 dove at high speed into a forest.

One pilot, 85 years old, an 11-time national gliding
champion, died in the crash of a sailplane shortly after
takeoff. According to witnesses, the glider "appeared to
be flying normally when it suddenly climbed abruptly
then nosed over into a steep dive and disappeared from

view in a forested area." The NTSB determined that the probable cause of the accident was "an incapacitating cardiac event," and noted the pilot's "poor decision to fly with known serious medical issues." Just six days before the accident the pilot had seen his cardiologist because he had experienced dizziness and left arm pain. The cardiologist had planned to schedule "left heart catheterization and possibly angioplasty in the next 1 to 2 weeks." But the pilot may have suspected for a long time that his medical condition was deteriorating, because he had not applied to renew his medical certificate — none is required for non-powered flight — since 1996.

It is always possible in such cases to trot out the platitude that "he died doing what he loved," but did the nightmare scenario ever end well for the passengers? Yes — once, in this ten-year period. Shortly after takeoff from North Las Vegas, the pilot of a Gulfstream 695A twin turboprop (formerly called a Turbo Commander) began to cough, put on an oxygen mask, turned back to the airport, and then lost consciousness. He had two passengers, neither of whom was a pilot. They managed, however, to turn off the autopilot, establish communication with the control tower, and bring the airplane back to the airport. After several aborted landing attempts, they pancaked the big twin onto the ground a few hundred feet short of the runway. The stricken pilot, who had not reported any cardiac issues on his medical applications, died after being taken to a hospital. The two passengers, who sustained some injuries, got out of the plane on their own — a rare happy ending in a decade of bad hearts and broken airplanes.

Ricky Nelson

Readers who allowed their children to tow them to the film "La Bamba," and some others of a certain age, are aware that in 1959 a singer named Ritchie Valens died, along with Buddy Holly and the self-styled Big Bopper, in the weather-related crash of a chartered Bonanza. The unhappy event was something of a milestone in the history of rock 'n' roll and was subsequently memorialized in a long, maudlin hit song called "The Day the Music Died." Chartered airplanes have been the undoing of many rock singers — more, perhaps, that even accidental overdoses. Jim Croce and Otis Redding died in airplane crashes; so, more recently, did Eric Hilliard Nelson, whom paleologists of television will remember as the crewcut younger brother, Ricky, in the series Ozzie and Harriet.

Nelson, his fiancée and all five members of his Stone
Canyon Band died when their DC-3, en route from
Guntersville, Alabama, to Dallas, caught fire in flight.
The airplane made a successful emergency landing in a
field near DeKalb, Texas, but only the pilot and copilot
escaped with their lives.

The accident sequence, as described by controllers and
witnesses on the ground, is simple. The flight left
Guntersville at 1:00 p.m. CST. At 5:08, one of the
crewmembers radioed to Fort Worth Center, with
understatement characteristic of pilots in dire
emergencies, "I think I'd like to turn around, head for
Texarkana here, I've got a little problem."

Several transmissions regarding headings and distances
to various possible landing places followed. At 5:11
came the last transmission received from the airplane:
"...smoke in the cockpit, have smoke in the cockpit." At
5:12, radar showed the DC-3 600 feet above the ground.
Radar contact was lost two minutes later.

Witnesses saw the airplane line up with a farm field out
of a descending left turn. It was trailing smoke, and bits
of falling debris ignited small grass fires in its wake. It
struck and severed power lines before landing, gear
down, in the field, where it plowed through some trees
before coming to rest. Both pilots escaped, seriously
injured, through the cockpit windows; but none of the
passengers got out. Fire, initially confined to the right

side of the cabin, eventually consumed most of the airplane.

National Transportation Safety Board investigators were able to determine from the debris that dropped from the airplane during its landing approach and from the charred fuselage itself that the fire most likely started in the right rear portion of the cabin, where the gasoline-fired cabin heater was located. The heater itself was too badly damaged, however, to reveal a source of ignition. Investigators therefore relied on the testimony of the pilots to piece together the sequence of events that preceded the accident.

The two pilots' accounts of the flight, though given under oath, were notably divergent. According to the captain, he went back to the cabin at one point during the flight to attend to the passengers and noticed smoke in the area occupied by Nelson and his fiancée. He checked the cabin heater and found its fire shield cool to the touch. Seeing no evidence of smoke or fire coming from the heater, he nevertheless activated one of its two built-in fire extinguishers and then opened the fresh-air inlets on his way back through the cabin. When he returned to the cockpit, the copilot was already discussing landing places with Center. The captain opened his cockpit window and the smoke increased. "Things rapidly got worse...I started a slow descending turn...and the window was open, and from there, things went completely blacked out. The smoke came through the cabin...it stained the windows, the cockpit glass, everything..."

He leaned through the open window to land. After the airplane had stopped and he had climbed out, the captain said, he went back to the boarding door and opened it.. He could see into the smoky interior, he said. There was a small fire in the area where he had originally seen smoke, but no one answered his calls; so he left to search for the passengers.

The copilot testified differently. After takeoff, the cabin heater began to "act up," showing an overheat light in the cockpit despite repeated resets. After a number of unsuccessful attempts to make the heater work properly from the cockpit, the captain went to the passenger cabin several times to try to solve the problem. "He signaled for me to turn it on or he...came up front and told me to turn it on or whatever. This happened several times. One of the times I refused to turn it on. I was getting nervous. I didn't think we should be messing with that heater en route. I had discussed this with [the captain] on previous flights...he turned it on again... Once, again, it either shut off or the overheat light came on, [it] went through the same cycle... The last time [the captain] went aft to the tail, he was aft for not very long, came out and signaled me to turn it on again, which I did. Several minutes after that, [a passenger]...came forward to me and said, 'There is smoke, back here in the cabin.' "

After the emergency landing, the copilot climbed out through the right cockpit window and fell to the ground. There was no fire on the outside of the right side of the airplane, but "the cabin of the aircraft through the windows appeared to be an inferno. Flames and smoke were all that one could see." Fearing an explosion, the copilot moved away from the airplane. He encountered the captain. "Don't tell anyone about the heater," the captain said. "Don't tell anyone about the heater..."

The NTSB concluded that, though it was impossible to pinpoint the source of the fire from material evidence, the copilot's testimony suggested that the captain's attempts to troubleshoot the cabin heater in flight had "apparently resulted in a fire" in or near the heater. The Board admitted that other sources of ignition were possible, including "careless smoking or other activity" in the cabin. It did not specify what "other activity" it had in mind.

The Board noted, however, that whatever the source of ignition might have been, the captain had failed to follow recommended emergency procedures for an in-flight fire. These included closing the fresh-air vents rather than opening them; instructing the passengers to begin using supplemental oxygen (which was available); and fighting the fire with the fire extinguisher that was in the cockpit. Since it was most likely smoke inhalation that killed or incapacitated the passengers, using oxygen might have enabled some to escape.

The captain's testimony that after he opened the cockpit window "things rapidly got worse" is worth remembering. In general, areas of expanding cross section and curvature on a fuselage are subject to low pressure. Internal spaces are usually at a pressure equal to or higher than ambient. Open cockpit windows therefore pull air out of the cockpit rather than allowing fresh air in. The air that enters the cockpit to replace that which is drawn out comes from the after part of the fuselage. Thus, opening the cockpit windows on the DC-3 was most likely responsible for the cockpit filling rapidly with smoke. Ventilating the fuselage also probably made conditions in the passenger cabin worse.

In-flight fire is terrifying but uncommon. When it occurs, there is little time to take action. Since it's difficult to think clearly in a cockpit full of smoke, pilots must consider their reactions to a fire in advance. The steps outlined in the emergency procedures section of the flight manual should be memorized. There is valuable insight and experience contained in actions that may appear counterintuitive, such as closing the air vents when smoke is detected.

Above all, time is of the essence. At the first suspicion of fire or smoke the pilot should begin a descent before doing anything else. If fire breaks out, every second will count. If it turns out to be a false alarm, pilots can console themselves with the reflection that regaining lost altitude is a minor inconvenience compared with being burned alive.

By the Book

The November, 2001 crash of American Airlines Flight 587, shortly after takeoff from JFK, sent a tremor through the aviation community. It involved an extremely rare event: the complete separation of one of the major flying surfaces — namely, the vertical stabilizer — of the airplane, an Airbus A300-600. In the ensuing loss of control, the engines also broke away from the airplane, which crashed on Long Island, killing all 265 persons aboard.

According to the National Transportation Safety Board's report on the accident, only one other commercial airliner, a Boeing 707 that broke apart in severe turbulence near Mt. Fuji in 1975, has ever lost a vertical fin in flight from external causes. That 707 encountered mountain wave turbulence so violent that the airplane broke into a number of pieces before reaching the ground, and a US Navy aircraft sent to investigate encountered gust accelerations far outside the flight envelope of any airliner. In the case of the Airbus, however, extreme turbulence was not a factor. The closest thing to it was the wake of a 747 five miles distant. Such a wake can give even a large airliner a pretty good thump, but cannot tear it apart.

The finding of the NTSB was that the first officer, who was the pilot flying, used inappropriately vigorous, rapidly alternating rudder inputs in response to the wake encounter. Normally, jet pilots stay off the rudders; but this particular pilot, according to one captain who had flown with him, had shown an inclination to overuse them. (On the other hand, some described him as an above-average pilot who never flew airplanes aggressively, but rather "smoothly and accurately.")

Two other factors were thought to have contributed to the overcontrol. One was the design of the A300-600's rudder control system, which provided very little force feedback. In fact, the additional force needed to drive a pedal to its stop at 250 knots is less than the 22-lb breakout force — intended to prevent inadvertent rudder movements — that must be applied in order to move the pedal in the first place. A survey of airline airplanes found none with rudder forces lower than those of the A300. Most other Airbus models, however, including the big four-engine A340, have characteristics similar to those of the A300-600, while Boeing and McDonnell-

Douglas models without exception have lower breakout forces and considerably higher deflection forces.

Airbus had deliberately reduced the rudder forces when it developed the A300-600, as compared with the earlier A300B2/B4, in order to keep them in harmony with reduced roll forces. It also replaced the earlier model's variable-ratio rudder travel limiter, which allows less and less rudder travel in response to the same amount of pedal travel as speed increases, with a simpler variable-stop system. One of the consequences of the change was that as speed increased, the pedal travel shrank and the force required to achieve the maximum allowable rudder deflection decreased. In effect, the sensitivity of the rudder pedals increased with speed. The fleet standards manager of American Airlines' Airbus 300 fleet told the NTSB that he "did not think that any pilot would have thought that full rudder could be gained from about 1 1/4 inch of pedal movement and 10 pounds of pressure (above the breakout force) at an airspeed of 250 knots."

Another possible contributing factor, according to the Board, was a simulator routine intended to train American's pilots for recovery from upsets. One demonstration case required a bank angle of more than 90 degrees, but the simulator could not be made to reach that angle if the pilot reacted promptly when the upset began. The simulator was consequently reprogrammed to make it unresponsive to the rudder until it attained the extreme bank angle. This artificial suspension of rudder effectiveness, the Board thought, might have instilled in this first officer — and possibly in other pilots — a sense that the real airplane would be similarly unresponsive, and that swift and vigorous rudder action would be needed to arrest any incipient upset.

The most significant finding to emerge from the accident, apart from the stated probable cause, was that the FAA's right hand didn't know what its left hand was doing. The NTSB reported that the fin failed at a load about one-third higher than that required for certification; thus, Airbus was blameless. Pilots, on the other hand, found it inexplicable that any aerodynamic load could cause a failure in an airplane flying under V_A, the maneuvering speed. By and large, pilots believed that you can't break an airplane at or below V_A. They had good reason for thinking so. The FAA's own *Pilot's Handbook of Aeronautical Knowledge* says that "any combination of flight control usage, including full deflection of the controls, or gust loads created by turbulence should not create an excessive air load if the airplane is operated below [the] maneuvering speed." FAR Part 25 contained a requirement that pilots be made aware that "full application of rudder and aileron controls ... should be confined to speeds below" the maneuvering speed — a declaration that does not state, but that most people would understand to imply, that such control applications below the maneuvering speed would not tear the airplane apart.

Various experts at American Airlines told the Board that they had always believed that V_A provided absolute structural protection. American had, furthermore, incorporated into its "Advanced Aircraft Maneuvering Program," which was intended to teach pilots how to recover from upsets and unusual attitudes, the advice that rudder rather than ailerons/spoilers should be used in certain circumstances, together with the implication that unusual attitudes were most likely to occur as a result of wake encounters; but there was no guidance on the possible effects of rapid rudder reversals. Evidence existed that this program had had an influence on the accident first officer's flying technique. Another document, the *Airplane Upset Recovery Training Aid*, prepared cooperatively by airframe manufacturers and a number of airlines, had also emphasized the use of rudder in unusual-attitude recoveries. Airbus had criticized it, not on structural grounds, however, but because unwary use of the rudder could lead to spins. Incidentally, Airbus also expressed doubts about the realism of simulators — another issue that would later play a part in this accident investigation.

The overstress protection that exists at V_A is, in fact, limited; but even the FAA itself seems to have been confused about what kind of protection V_A actually provides. It was as though the engineers who design airplanes, the bureaucrats who certify them, and the pilots who fly them existed in different worlds, separated by membranes impermeable to information. But that isn't the case. Some pilots are aeronautical engineers, and all airframe manufacturers, and the FAA, employ pilots. The misconceptions about V_A that pervaded the flying community may have been news to the NTSB, but no one can suggest that were unknown to the airframe manufacturers.

One of two steps needed to be taken. Either the manufacturers had to build their airplanes to match the *beliefs* of the users regarding maneuvering speed, not just the technical requirements of the FARs, or else some effort had to be made either to re-educate pilots or to re-define the maneuvering speed so that it would play the role expected of it. Neither of these steps was taken prior to this accident.

The plain fact is that the whole concept of maneuvering speed is pointless if the published speed does not provide complete protection. "Maneuvering speed" should be synonymous with "safe speed" — a speed at which air loads cannot blow the flying surfaces off an airplane regardless of its attitude. A maneuvering speed with hidden exceptions is simply a cruel fraud. What use is it? Well, it does have one use, as the case of AA587 demonstrates. It provides manufacturers with a shield to hide behind if one of their airplanes breaks when, by pilots' understanding of things, it shouldn't have.

Certification requirements for maneuvering speed assume the use of only one control at a time; for instance, they do not provide for simultaneous pitch-up and roll. Furthermore, as far as the fin and rudder are concerned, full rudder deflection is permitted only when no sideslip is present. In other words, if the airplane yaws you are not allowed to use full rudder to bring it back.

The aerodynamic concept underlying the FAR definition of maneuvering speed is a simple one. A flying surface can only provide a certain maximum lift coefficient before stalling, and the aerodynamic force experienced at that lift coefficient depends on the speed. The force exerted at the maneuvering speed is the so-called limit loading for which the wing structure is designed.

Nevertheless, that is really not the greatest force a wing can experience at the maneuvering speed. A limit-load pull-up combined with roll produces a still larger load, because the downward-deflected aileron, like a landing flap, increases the amount of lift the outer portion of the wing can produce while adding a large torsional, or twisting, component. Similarly, anti-yaw rudder applied when the airplane is in a sideslip — this was what broke the Airbus's fin — produces a larger load than the fin would experience with the rudder aligned with it. To be sure, it is difficult to apply rudder against sideslip, because the airplane begins to stabilize itself before the pilot can react. The theory in the case of AA587 is that the pilot got into phase with the airplane in such a way that, with the help of the Airbus's unusually sensitive rudder pedals, he managed to apply full rudder at just the worst possible moment. His case was not unique; the NTSB enumerated six previous instances of upsets in Airbus aircraft in which fin stresses had exceeded the design ultimate load. None involved the A300B2/B4 with the variable-ratio rudder limiter.

It might seem desirable to change certification requirements so as to require sufficient structural strength to withstand all control deflections in all attitudes at the maneuvering speed. Airframe manufacturers might resist such changes, however, because they would require heavier structures and thus raise the operating costs of future models, and would represent a massive and costly remedy for a statistically minor problem. An alternative to structural changes might be fly-by-wire control systems, which many Airbus models, but not the A300, already incorporate. Fly-by-wire systems can be programmed to hold structural loads within acceptable boundaries.

For existing aircraft, two changes could be contemplated. One would be to lower the published V_A to a level at which all possible maneuvers are protected. If the loads experienced by AA587's fin be taken as a guide, the speed reduction would be on the order of ten percent. Of course, even redefined V-speeds would not necessarily change the speeds at which airplanes are actually flown. AA587 was not flying at 250 knots in order to stay below V_A, but to observe the speed limit below 10,000 feet. But they would make the meaning of V_A more clear, and the implications of certain combinations of control movements more apparent to pilots.

The other change, which has already been set in motion by this accident and will continue, is to re-educate pilots about what V_A means for airplanes that currently exist. Still, the most re-educated pilot in the world may forget what he knows when his airplane is flipped over at low altitude by a wake turbulence encounter, or if he thinks it's about to be.

At Least Upside Down We're Flyin'

In September, 1997, an Alaska Airlines MD-83, N963AS, received a C check, an inspection and maintenance operation that occurred at intervals of 15 months or about 4,800 flight hours. In the course of the C check, a mechanic found that the end play in the screw jack controlling the incidence of the horizontal stabilizer, and therefore the airplane's longitudinal trim, was 40 thousandths of an inch.

The Alaska Airlines maintenance instructions for checking the end play of the trim jackscrew contained the following passage:

"Check that end play limits are between .003 and .040 inch. Readings in excess of the above are cause for replacement..."

These directions are confusing if the reading is exactly .040, which is neither "between" .003 and .040 nor "in excess" of .040. Taking the first sentence literally, however, the mechanic performing the check made out a "nonroutine work card" calling for replacement of the jackscrew assembly.

Three days later another mechanic, aware that jackscrew assemblies were expensive and hard to come by, repeated the end-play check several times and arrived at a reading of .033 inch. The airplane was returned to service. No further action was taken, although even at the normally expected wear rate of one thousandth of an inch per 1,000 flight hours, the trim jack would be out of limits by the time the next end-play measurement, performed only on alternate C checks, took place.

Maintenance of the MD-83 includes regular greasing of the jackscrew. This was a time-consuming and messy procedure that required opening a small inspection plate at the tip of the T-tail, pressure-greasing the jackscrew nut, manually smearing the exposed portions of the jackscrew with grease, and cycling the trim several times to distribute the fresh grease evenly over the threads.

The jackscrew assembly is the only structural component securing the leading edge of the horizontal stabilizer.

Many airplanes have two of them, but the MD-80 series uses only one, achieving redundancy by means of a second tube within the hollow jackscrew. Failure of either the tube or the jackscrew simply shifts the load to the other.

The outer surface of the steel jackscrew carries a double helix of massive square "acme" threads. It is capable of withstanding loads many times larger than those encountered in flight. Two motors drive it, one for primary trim, the other for the autopilot. The entire jackscrew and motor assembly is attached to the leading edge of the stabilizer torque box and rides up and down with it; the nut, mounted in a gimbal to allow it to align itself with the screw, is secured to the fin structure. Periodic endplay checks are intended to monitor wear of the jackscrew and nut.

In January, 2000, three months before the next end-play check of the jackscrew assembly was due, N963AS plunged into the Pacific Ocean off the coast of California. When the wreckage was recovered, wire-like fragments of material were found adhering to the jackscrew, which was separated from its nut. The nut, which was also recovered, was completely stripped; the material clinging to the jackscrew was the last residue of the nut's threads, worn down to thin shards. The jackscrew shaft, free to slide up and down through the nut once the threads failed, had eventually broken through its lower stop, plunging the airplane into an inverted dive from which recovery was impossible.

Investigators examined the jackscrew carefully. There was no sign of fresh grease on it, nor on the nut, except in the clogged passages of the grease fitting, where minute traces were found. This was true in other lubricated assemblies in the empennage as well. Since grease is impervious to sea water, it was evident that the prescribed lubrication procedure had not been followed, even though the airplane's maintenance records indicated that the work had been performed at the prescribed intervals. The botched job was traced to a single mechanic at the airline's San Francisco maintenance facility. It turned out, furthermore, that two other Alaska Airlines airplanes that had exhibited abnormal jackscrew wear had been serviced by the same mechanic.

The National Transportation Safety Board criticized Alaska Airlines and the FAA for extending the intervals between both lubrications and end play checks, noting that more frequent end play checks would have provided an opportunity to assess the adequacy of less frequent lubrication. The Board also said that the absence on the MD-80 series airplanes of a "fail-safe mechanism to prevent the catastrophic effects of total acme thread loss" had contributed to the accident. In fairness to the designers of the airplane, however, it must be said that with proper inspection and maintenance, total loss of the threads could never occur.

Although the Board placed responsibility for the accident with Alaska Airlines' maintenance practices, much of its

235-page report dealt with crew actions leading up to the final failure. The flight, which originated in Puerto Vallarta, Mexico, was bound for Seattle-Tacoma with a stop in San Francisco. The electric pitch trim jammed during the initial climb, and the autopilot disconnected when it sensed that it was having to apply excessive up elevator to counteract the mistrim. After leveling out at FL 310, the crew hand-flew the airplane, applying a total of about 30 pounds of pulling force to the two control columns combined, for 24 minutes. They then increased speed, and continued to hand-fly for one hour and 22 minutes using ten pounds of back pressure before re-engaging the autopilot.

The crew contacted the airline's maintenance and dispatch control center at Seattle to discuss a precautionary landing at Los Angeles. At this point the crew had presumably been struggling with the jammed trim, while hand-flying the airplane, for a long time. The captain, perceiving that the dispatcher was pressuring him to continue to San Francisco, commented to a flight attendant, "It just blows me away that they think we're gonna land, they're gonna fix it, now they're worried about the flow. I'm sorry, this airplane's not gonna go anywhere for a while."

Eventually the captain and the Seattle dispatcher agreed that the airplane would land at Los Angeles. There followed a discussion with a mechanic at LAX during which the captain said that they had tried everything to overcome the jam, and nothing had worked. "If you've got any hidden circuit breakers," he joked, "we'd love to know about 'em."

At this point — it was 4:09 local time — the airplane was over the channel between Los Angeles and Santa Catalina Island, still at FL 310. As often happens when a pilot is reviewing for a mechanic the efforts he has made to correct some problem, the captain decided to have one more try. He disengaged the autopilot and applied the nose-up trim controls. Now, for unknown reasons, the jam freed itself. A moment later the last scraps of thread holding the nut in place on the jackscrew sheared off, and the screw slid upward through the nut. The stabilizer stopped at a positive — that is, aircraft nose down — setting of 2.5 degrees, and the airplane entered a steep dive. The captain transmitted to ATC, "We are in a dive here...we've lost vertical control of our airplane." Applying between 130 and 140 pounds of pull to the controls, the crew recovered from the dive forty seconds after it began, having lost more than 7,000 feet.

The captain now requested a block altitude, telling the center controller, "We're gonna do a little troubleshooting." He discussed the situation with the first officer, commenting, "We're in much worse shape now... can it go any worse?...it probably can..." Never imagining that the primary structure of the trim mechanism had failed, the crew interpreted the situation as a trim runaway to fully or almost fully nose down.

Three minutes after the initial dive, the captain addressed the presumably disconcerted, if not absolutely terrified, passengers over the PA system. "Folks, we have a flight control problem up front here. We're working on it. That's Los Angeles off to the right there, that's where we're intending to go. We're pretty busy up here working this situation. I don't anticipate any big problems once we get a couple of sub-systems on the line, but we will be going into LAX and I'd anticipate us parking there in about 20 to 30 minutes."

"Slow it down and see what happens," the captain said to the first officer, who was the pilot flying. He then told Center that he wanted to descend to 10,000 feet. The first officer, no doubt mindful of the unnerving result of their last experiment, suggested that they stay where they were.

ATC cleared the flight to descend to 17,000 feet. A flight attendant come to the cockpit and reported, "We had like a big bang back there." "I think the stab trim thing is broke," the captain explained, and then asked the flight attendant to secure the cabin and make sure everybody was "strapped in," because he intended to "unload" the tail — that is, allow the airplane to pitch over again.

The crew now extended the slats and eleven degrees of flap. The airplane was indicating 250 kts. The captain said to the first officer, "It's pretty stable right here, but we got to get down to 180."

He then asked the first officer to retract the flaps and slats. "What I wanna do," he went on, " is get the nose up, and then let the nose fall through and see if we can stab it when it's unloaded." This is one of the few actions of the crew that the Safety Board criticized. Observing that "without clearer guidance to flight crews regarding which actions are appropriate and which are inappropriate in the event of an inoperative or malfunctioning flight control system, pilots may experiment with improvised troubleshooting measures that could inadvertently worsen the condition of a controllable airplane," the Board suggested that "flight crews dealing with an in-flight control problem should maintain any configuration that would aid in accomplishing a safe approach and landing, unless that configuration change adversely affects the airplane's controllability." In other words, once the flaps and slats were out, they should have stayed out.

The first officer, evidently uneasy with the captain's interest in continued experimentation, said, "I think if it's controllable, we oughta just try to land it." The captain, who may also have had misgivings about further efforts to restore the trim to operation, was easily persuaded. "You think so?" he said. "Okay, let's head for LA."

A few seconds later, there was a faint thump. "You feel that?" said the first officer.

"Yeah," said the captain. "Okay, gimme [unintelligible word] — see, this is a bitch." Probably the captain was referring to the force needed to hold the nose up. The cockpit area microphone picked up a sound like that of the slat/flap handle moving, followed, a few seconds later, by an extremely loud noise. It was the noise of the jackscrew's bottom stop failing, the fin fairing being torn loose, and the stabilizer flipping up to an aerodynamically disastrous angle.

The jet entered a steep dive and rolled over onto its back. In this attitude it was stable. All the way down, the captain struggled heroically to recover control:

"Push and roll, push and roll! Okay, we are inverted... and now we gotta get it...push, push, push...push the blue side up...push...okay, now let's kick rudder, left rudder, left rudder!"

The first officer could not reach the left rudder pedal.

"Okay, right rudder, right rudder. Are we flyin'?...we're flyin'...we're flyin'...tell 'em what we're doin'...gotta get it over again...at least upside down we're flyin'."

A series of compressor stalls began and the engines spooled down. The captain called for speed brakes. The airplane was dropping at 15,000 feet a minute. Just before the impact with the ocean the captain said, "Ah, here we go!"

Almost on Top

Early on a Sunday afternoon in June the pilot of a K35 Bonanza called the Boise, Idaho, Flight Service Station for a weather briefing. His destination was Burbank, in southern California.

"Okay," the briefer said, but that was the last good news he had to offer. "VFR flight is not recommended." There were flight precautions for moderate to occasionally severe icing between 8,000 and 20,000 feet along the entire route, and, as if that weren't enough, "...moderate to isolated severe turbulence below 20,000, mountain obscuration, and IFR conditions in clouds, precipitation, and fog...Right now enroute ceilings are varied from 1,000 feet to 10,000 feet broken to overcast, visibilities from three to seven miles in rain and snow showers and fog all up along that route."

"Could you tell me if I could take a route to Oregon, to the west from here?" the pilot asked. But the conditions were the same in that direction.

The terrain between Grangeville, Idaho, where the pilot was, and Burbank is almost uniformly mountainous, unpopulated and, under bad weather conditions, forbidding. On the other hand, the forecast of 1,000-foot ceilings and three-mile visibilities — VFR conditions — may have sounded encouraging — sufficiently encouraging, evidently, that at some point not long after receiving the briefing the pilot took off from Grangeville.

His first radio contact, about 70 minutes after the end of the weather briefing, was with Boise Tower. For the next 20 minutes he remained in contact with Boise and Mountain Home Air Force Base Approach Control. It's not clear from the National Transportation Safety Board's account of the accident (which is unusually sketchy) whether or not the private pilot had an instrument rating, but it appears that he did not, and that he intended to conduct the flight under VFR. Conditions must have proved worse than he expected, however, because at 2:47 PDT he asked Mountain Home for a different altitude and a change of destination to Elko, Nevada. Whether he was flying under a clearance at this point the accident report does not make clear.

Mountain Home handed the plane off to Salt Lake City Center at 2:58. It was then at an altitude of 11,800 feet. At 3:20, the pilot reported that he was at 13,500 feet.

Twenty-five minutes later, Center told him that flights landing at Elko were having to make instrument approaches, whereupon he changed his destination back to Burbank.

At 4:26, the pilot declared an emergency to Salt Lake Center. In a series of partly unintelligible transmissions he said, in effect, "It's an emergency, I have severe icing and cannot maintain altitude."

The pilot asked for vectors "so I can get out of these clouds." The controller responded with a new heading, and a minute later the pilot reported that he was gaining altitude. The controller asked whether he was still in clouds, and he replied, "Yes, but it's getting a little clearer."

The controller continued to talk with the pilot. At 4:33, he said, "...how is your icing now?" The pilot replied, "I am almost [unintelligible] the clouds but there is still some icing." Presumably the unintelligible phrase was "above" or "out of." Two minutes later, the pilot reported, "I am right now breaking out."

That was his last transmission. The controller tried in vain to re-establish contact with him, and then reported that the airplane had disappeared from radar. The wreckage was located by the Civil Air Patrol the next day, 20 miles north of Eureka, Nevada, at an elevation of around 6,000 feet. Portions of the surrounding terrain rose above 10,000 feet.

Accidents of this category — attempted VFR flight in marginal weather conditions — account for many general aviation fatalities. Two aspects of such accidents are of interest: the decision-making process that got the pilot into the situation in the first place, and the circumstances immediately surrounding the final loss of control or collision with terrain.

The decision to go or not to go may have been influenced, in this case and in many others, by the day of the week. It was Sunday. The pilot may have felt that he had to be somewhere on Monday; we don't know. Whatever may have been the situation of this particular pilot, it often seems as if some pilots involved in accidents had put undue pressure on themselves either to make a long-planned trip (accident on Friday) or to get back home (accident on Sunday).

In any case, it's evident that he very much wanted to go. The weather forecast was unpromising. Thousand-foot ceilings and three-mile visibilities sound fairly good if you happen to be in the Midwest. In the mountains their significance is different. Weather observations are taken at cities and at airports, which are usually build in low-lying regions. The route from Grangeville to Burbank lay almost entirely over high-altitude wilderness. The weather conditions between reporting points could only be guessed at, but "clouds, precipitation and fog" gave a hint of what might be expected.

The forecast of icing up to 20,000 feet meant that the clouds went at least that high; there is no icing outside clouds. In mountainous regions, however, cloud cover is often irregular, tending to collect around peaks and ridges. It's likely that the local conditions at Grangeville were good enough to encourage the pilot to think that he could climb to on top and find his way southward between buildups.

Once the Bonanza was airborne and southbound, the stage was set for a predictable sequence of events. The cloud tops rise imperceptibly higher. The pilot — like a hiker surmounting a series of ridges who believes each to be the last until he reaches its summit and sees a still higher ridge beyond — crosses one swirling white hill after another, veering from side to side to pass through the valleys between them, and finding himself forced gradually upward.

By the time the pilot contacted Boise Tower, he was probably becoming a little anxious. Under his particular circumstances, there was not a lot that controllers on the ground could do for him; controllers can sometimes vector you around areas of severe weather (and specifically of heavy precipitation, which they can see on their radar), but they have no way to keep you VFR on a cloudy day. It's not clear that the pilot realized this; his later request for a vector "so I can get out of these clouds" implies a belief that controllers could do more for him than they really could.

When he changed his destination to Elko he had
evidently begun to feel that the weather was worse than
he had anticipated and that he ought to get onto the
ground. When he learned that he would have to make an
instrument approach at Elko, however, he decided to
continue to Burbank. Presumably he was not instrument
rated, did not have instrument charts, and so could not
make an instrument approach.

At some point, he flew into the clouds. By 4:26, when he
suddenly declared an icing emergency, he had been
airborne for more than two hours and had been at oxygen
altitudes for an hour. He was probably under great stress.
If he was not an experienced instrument pilot, his report
of "severe" icing cannot be taken at fact value, especially
in light of the fact that shortly after reporting it he was
able to establish a positive climb rate; severely iced
reciprocating-engine airplanes do not climb.
Nevertheless, it felt severe to him, and that feeling
probably played a part in his undoing.

As the airplane climbed, the pilot perceived that it was
"getting a little clearer." Evidently he was near the cloud
tops. The airplane would have been climbing slowly. Ice
accumulation is often most rapid near the tops of clouds,
but the pilot's radio communications referred only to
"some icing," and it's not clear whether he meant that ice
was still accumulating or only that there was still visible
ice on the airplane.

He was now at an extremely critical juncture. It is almost certain that, motivated by a desperate desire to get back into clear air, he was trying to coax the airplane upward. His airspeed was probably low. His rate of climb was probably fluctuating because of random air movements near the tops of the clouds, and the light toward which he was clawing probably faded and brightened as he passed beneath lower and higher portions of the cloud tops. "I am right now breaking out," he said in his last transmission. He probably felt that the elusive tops were just within reach, if he could only coax a little more climb out of the airplane...

And then, most likely, the airplane stalled. Even a small accumulation of rime ice on the leading edges would have pushed the stalling speed closer to the best rate of climb speed, whereas the pilot's impatience to get out of the imprisoning clouds could have driven him to ever-lower indicated airspeeds. An inadvertent stall-spin, which puts little stress on the airplane but a great deal on the pilot, is the most likely explanation for the fact that the airplane was apparently still intact when it collided with the ground.

The phrase "VFR not recommended" and the guidelines for its use are the distillation of lessons learned from many years of accidents involving VFR pilots in bad weather. It is true that many pilots have ignored the warning and have reached their destinations safely. Any such flight is a gamble; the player sometimes — probably most of the time — wins. But the sequence of events leading to a fatal accident often has unexpected twists and turns. Most likely this pilot never imagined, when he took off, that in two and a half hours he would find himself iced up, in clouds, and perhaps hypoxic, and that he would end his life in a stall-spin. If you had suggested that possibility to him, he would have said that he would never let things go that far — he would turn back first. But he didn't turn back. Why not? You'd have to be there to know — and that's why the "VFR not recommended" warning is so often ignored.

Experiments

As "experimental/amateur-built" airplanes become more numerous, they naturally figure more prominently in the accident statistics. As you might expect, they are more prone to accidents arising from design or construction errors than certified airplanes are. A look at their fatal accidents for a single month — July, 2001 — reveals this pattern and others as well.

The first accident occurred on July 2. A Challenger II, a tandem two-seat ultralight with a high wing and engine and a low boom supporting the empennage, struck trees during an attempted return to the airport when its engine failed shortly after takeoff. The pilot had bought the airplane from its builder and had flown it very little — reportedly only two hours in the past year, and not at all within the past three or four months. Although it had been registered, the N number was not painted on the

airplane, and the required data plate was also absent.
According to FAA records, in fact, it had never been
licensed.

A witness to the accident, who had flown the airplane
himself, said that when he flew it it had a "severe yaw
problem," and he had been afraid to fly it again. Weak
directional stability is a known characteristic of the
Challenger II with doors in place; it requires a good deal
of attention to the rudder. The owner had added some
vertical stabilizer area and a trim tab and had removed
the doors, having been advised that doing so would
alleviate the directional stability problem. The reason for
the engine failure could not be found, but the pattern of
the accident was classic enough; turnbacks with
insufficient altitude have claimed the lives of countless
pilots. The NTSB attributed the accident to the 100-hour
pilot's lack of familiarity with the airplane.

On July 14, a Mohawk 1, another ultralight whose
configuration is similar to that of a Piper Cub, crashed on
the owner's first flight at the controls. Another pilot had
flown the airplane around the pattern earlier, but, finding
the elevator extremely sensitive and the rudder
ineffective, he returned to report that it was "OK for taxi,
but not safe to fly." The owner then went out to taxi it
and apparently became airborne inadvertently. He stalled
and spun about half a mile from the airstrip.

On the same day, a commercial pilot died when the BD-5
he was flying struck the ground at high speed, seemingly

under control. The NTSB has not yet determined a probable cause of the accident, and few details are available. There was a witness, however, who was himself a pilot. He was driving down a highway when he saw the BD-5 cross in front of him in a climb, then turn back and head toward him, "moving really fast for its size." He noted that the airplane "weaved up and down, as well as left and right" as it approached. It struck the ground 50 yards in front of him, nose low and in a slight left turn, and immediately exploded.

Another accident for which a probable cause has not yet been determined involved a VariEze that crashed, with two aboard, near Palm Springs, California on July 20. The canard surface was missing from the debris field; it was located several days later half a mile from the accident site, having apparently separated from the airplane in flight.

On July 21, a Kelly-D biplane lost its right upper wing panel while performing aerobatics that a witness characterized as "smooth" and probably not involving more than a mild 3.5 Gs. Examination of the wreckage revealed loose jam nuts on half a dozen bracing wires and an improperly glued wooden doubler on the wing spar, although it is not clear from the NTSB report whether what failed was the doubler or the spar itself. At the time of the accident, the airplane, which had been licensed in May, 2000, and had logged 60 hours, was for sale. The owner had bought the incomplete project in 1997 from another builder, who had begun it in 1984.

Two days later, another biplane crashed, this one an 85%
replica of a Curtiss F-IIC-2 Goshawk, a vintage biplane
fighter and dive bomber. The amateur-built airplane,
which had never before flown, was equipped with a nine-
cylinder, 280-hp Lycoming R-680 radial engine. Near the
end of what was supposed to be a taxi test on the runway,
the engine surged and the airplane became airborne,
veered to the left, stalled and crashed, killing the front-
seat builder-pilot. The rear-seat passenger, a 9,000-hour
ATP, who survived, told investigators that he had had no
intention of flying in the airplane, which in his opinion
was unsafe because "the ailerons did not have full travel
and the strakes [sic] were hitting the flying wires." It
appeared that the surging of the engine might have been
due to a buildup of oil residue on the propeller governor
drive shaft, which caused it to stick. Post-mortem
examination of the pilot revealed residues of Tylenol and
Benadryl in his blood. Benadryl, which is usually taken
to relieve allergies, was found by one medical study to
have a more adverse effect on driving performance than
alcohol. The NTSB report does not specify the amount of
each substance needed to achieve similar results.

On July 24, a Giles G-202, a competition aerobatic
airplane, apparently stalled and spun while arriving at
Wittman field at Oshkosh, Wisconsin for the big EAA
fly-in commercially known as AirVenture. The pilot,
who flew for a major airline and had nearly 22,000
hours, had previously owned a Pitts, had flown an Extra
for a couple of hours before flying the Giles, and had

logged 35 hours in the Giles. The NTSB attributed the accident to his relative lack of familiarity with the airplane, although 35 hours seems like enough to create familiarity in a highly experienced pilot. A Cherokee pilot who had followed the Giles on the way into Wittman Field said that it was flying about 90 mph and was very nose high; but airplanes designed for inverted flight, with symmetrical airfoils and zero wing incidence, naturally appear nose-high when flying slowly, and 90 mph is not excessively slow for an airplane with as low a wing loading — probably around 15 lb/sq ft — as the Giles has when flown single-pilot.

On the same day, a Kolb SlingShot, a pusher ultralight similar in configuration to the Challenger, crashed out of a stall-spin while attempting a dead-stick forced landing. The cause of the accident was fuel starvation, according to investigators, who determined that the cut-off end of a loose fuel vent line was free to come into contact with a flexible neoprene pad, forming an airtight seal and choking off fuel flow to the engine.

On July 26, a Glasair III approaching Wittman Field stalled and spun while making S-turns for spacing on final approach. Accident investigators found no anomalies in the airframe or engine. Oddly enough, however, the lawyer whom the pilot's family hired to sue a company that had recently performed maintenance on the engine was named Stephen Lawyer.

Two days later, the non-pilot owner of a Barnett J4B gyroplane, who had omitted to "hang" the aircraft from its rotor mast to determine its balance characteristics, found it to be nose-heavy on his first flight. He corrected this situation — the accident report does not say how — and flew again, this time for about an hour. Returning to the field, he lost control of the craft and crashed. The NTSB attributed the accident to his inexperience, but implied that noseheaviness might have had something to do with it.

On July 30, a Glastar, a high-wing, fixed-gear airplane, crashed vertically into mountainous terrain when its 68-year-old pilot lost control for undetermined reasons while cruising at around 13,000 feet on the way back from Oshkosh. Investigators thought the electric trim actuator might have been in the full nose-down position. The pilot's son-in-law reported that he had complained of shortness of breath a week earlier. The NTSB report does not mention hypoxia as a possible factor, though it does come to mind.

The next, and last, day of that month, a Lancair 360 with the owner-builder and a flight instructor aboard flew into an area of level three to level five thunderstorms off the coast of Georgia. The flight was conducted under IFR, and a radar controller had repeatedly warned the pilot of heavy weather ahead. After the airplane disappeared from radar, a Coast Guard search plane located floating debris on the ocean surface. The body of the owner was recovered, but that of the instructor, who had been technically the pilot in command because the owner lacked a valid medical certificate, was not.

That was one month. True, it was a month with an unusual amount of amateur-built activity, what with good summer weather and the Oshkosh fly-in. The accidents I have described were all fatal; there were also various non-fatal accidents and incidents involving amateur-built types. It is striking, however, that the proportion of homebuilts among the fatal accidents is considerably higher than among the non-fatal ones. The NTSB lists 283 accidents and incidents that month; 42 of these involved homebuilts. Fifty of the accidents involved one or more fatalities; twelve of these involved homebuilts. In other words, 30 of 233 non-fatal accidents involved homebuilts, whereas 12 of 50 fatal ones did. In considering these statistics, the vastly larger number of hours flown by certified airplanes should be kept in mind.

What I find notable about the fatal accidents involving homebuilts is the relatively large proportion that occur on first flights or inadvertent flights, or involve inexperienced or unlicensed pilots; the high incidence of stall-spin or loss-of-control accidents; and the comparatively large number of events involving gross mechanical problems such as structural or engine failure or marginal flying qualities. And then there's the lack of caution: the persistence and self-reliance needed for building an airplane may become obstinacy and overconfidence when it's time to fly. It's doubtful that

202

much can be done about these problems. Amateur builders voluntarily turn their backs on the benefits provided by certification and professional construction and maintenance in order to experience an adventure and, when all goes well, a satisfaction, that are of a wholly different order from those of flying factory-built airplanes. Amateur builders replace the safeguards they have abandoned with a community, increasingly mediated by the internet, of mutual support and shared information, and certainly get greater enjoyment out of their communications with like-minded builder-pilots than the owners of factory planes get from receiving AD notices from the FAA.

No death is negligible; each is the extinction of a world. Some must be accepted as the price of not staying in bed; others appear poignantly, absurdly unnecessary. The operation of amateur-built airplanes entails a disproportionate number of the latter kind. In so many cases, the fatal outcome proceeds from some trivial piece of stupidity, ignorance, carelessness or momentary bravado. Nevertheless, surviving husbands, wives and children pay the price; to them it is probably cold comfort that the victim "died doing what he loved."

Breakup

It may be true, as the song says, that breaking up is hard to do. Still, with a little help from heavy weather and/or a less-than-adept pilot, it can sometimes be accomplished in the blink of an eye.

Two cases in point: first, a 7,000-hour ATP, descending between thunderstorms in a King Air, lost control of his airplane, which broke up as he tried to recover; second, the instrument-rated private pilot of an Allison turbine-powered Beech A36 became disoriented and entered a spiral dive. The second case ended like the first, with the in-flight breakup of the airplane. Two died in the King Air, four in the Bonanza.

The King Air was on a Part 135 flight across Florida on a June morning. Earlier, while filing his IFR flight plan, the pilot had been warned by the FSS specialist of thunderstorms along his route, including one "real heavy cell" in the Panama City area. Tops were as high as 48,000 feet. The briefer suggested that the pilot try to get some pilot reports; he replied he would, but added that the airplane was equipped with radar and a Stormscope, and he would also be able to get assistance with weather avoidance from en route controllers.

During the flight, a controller warned of "heavy precipitation from about 30 miles south of Panama City and it extends to about 20 east of Panama City and they extend northeastbound almost to the Seminole VORTAC." But the pilot was confident. "It looks like on our radar here," he said, "that [if] we go straight ahead we'll be all right..."

At 10:04 the flight, cruising at FL180, was cleared to descend to 16,000 feet. At 10:07 the controller broadcast a notice of a convective SIGMET to all pilots. Two minutes later, he cleared the King Air out of 16,000 for 11,000 and handed him off to Pensacola Approach.

Contacting Pensacola, the pilot requested and got a deviation "ten to fifteen degrees to the right for weather." What happened next is uncertain. Radar returns from the King Air showed it initially descending at about 2,500 feet per minute to 11,000 feet with a calculated airspeed of about 190 kias. Thirty seconds later it began a precipitous descent, dropping from 11,000 feet to 900 feet, where it was lost from radar, in only 47 seconds, for an average descent rate — not even the maximum attained — of over 13,000 fpm. Its airspeed increased to 265 kias at 10:13:25, then began to diminish again. At 10:13:52, the controller heard, from an unidentified source assumed to be the King Air, the words, "3,000 outta control and going down," followed, two seconds later, by a second utterance, this one unintelligible.

There were a few witnesses to the breakup. One reported seeing the airplane circle two or three times and hearing a strange noise coming from it, followed by two loud booms. Other witnesses also reported the booms — most likely coming from the wing spars, which failed outboard of the engine nacelles — and whistling sounds. Based on the radar data, a Beech accident investigator concluded that the airplane broke up at about 3,800 or 3,900 feet, both the horizontal tail and the wings failing downward. This is a classic pattern: the stabilizer fails from pilot-induced overload, and then, with the balancing tail downforce suddenly removed, the airplane pitches violently nose-down, overloading the wings with negative lift.

It's impossible to know exactly what the King Air encountered and how the onboard radar and Stormscope depicted it, if at all. Ground-based weather radar, scanning the area at 14-second intervals, showed no returns along the route of flight as little as a minute before the loss of control; the next two passes showed increasing echoes, which then disappeared. But at the time of the accident, it suddenly showed a Level 5 echo

— the most powerful category — that coincided with the last plotted point on the King Air's track.

Although the violent cell appeared with freakish suddenness, the National Transportation Safety Board put all the blame for the accident on the pilot, citing his "poor in-flight weather evaluation...operation of the airplane at an indicated airspeed greater than the design maneuvering speed in a thunderstorm contrary to the pilot's operating handbook...[and] failure to obtain in-flight weather advisories with any air traffic control facility before encountering the adverse weather."

The King Air's maneuvering speed is nominally 169 kias, but in this case it might have been slightly lower because there were only two people in the airplane; maneuvering speed diminishes with decreasing wing loading. Although the accident report seems to attribute the maximum calculated airspeed of 265 kias, well above the maximum operating speed of 208 kias, to pilot action, it occurred while the airplane was descending at 13,000 fpm, presumably in severe turbulence and out of control. Nevertheless, before the loss of control the King Air was already traveling at 190 kias — well above the maneuvering speed.

The case of the A36 was similar in some respects and quite different in others. The pilot was en route from Canada to South Carolina. He had made a stop in Buffalo, but had not obtained a fresh weather briefing there. The briefing he had obtained in Canada had

omitted mention of expected icing in clouds in the West
Virginia area; the briefer had offered to obtain
AIRMETs, which contained the information, but the pilot
had declined because it would have taken too long.

At the time of the accident he was on an instrument flight
plan, cruising at 13,000 feet in the area of forecast icing.
The accident unfolded with puzzling rapidity and in radio
silence. As recorded by ATC radar, the airplane turned
westward, accelerated rapidly to an indicated 242 kias
while descending, and broke up at 11,800 feet. Like the
King Air's, the Bonanza's wings and stabilizers both
failed downward, indicating pilot-induced overstress and
failure of the tail surfaces followed by failure of the wing
from negative overload. In this case, there was no
indication of turbulence that might have caused the loss
of control. The accident report doesn't mention whether
or not the airplane had an autopilot (a well-equipped A36
like this one normally would) or whether the autopilot
was engaged; nor does it mention the gyro instruments
and their power supply, natural suspects in an en route
upset.

Again the NTSB focused on the pilot, citing his "spatial
disorientation, his subsequent loss of control of the
airplane, and his overload of the horizontal stabilizer
during a recovery attempt." It continued, "Factors include
the pilot's continued flight into icing conditions, his lack
of airspeed control, and the lack of an AIRMET advisory
from the weather briefer." If the pilot did indeed
encounter icing, he didn't mention it to controllers, and

the NTSB does not propose an icing-related scenario that would lead from level flight to breakup in only 23 seconds.

The report dwells at length, however, on the pilot's history, which was colorful, to say the least. He had been flying for less than four years, but during that time had logged almost 1,500 hours. A radiologist by profession, he had at first failed both his private and instrument flight tests, but had passed both on rechecks. Two years before the accident, he had attended a formal training course for the turbine Bonanza. On arriving at the training site, the pilot had related to his instructor how he had encountered a thunderstorm on the way. He had lost 6,000 feet of altitude and the airplane had suffered hail damage, including holes in the radome that the instructor — like Doubting Thomas — could put his fingers through.

That wasn't all. Apparently possessed, like Coleridge's ancient mariner, by a compulsion to confess his sins, he had related that he had also landed at the wrong airport, believing it to be the training site. Touching down with a quartering tailwind of 15 knots, he had run off the runway and into the grass. He had gone on to tell the instructor that one reason he was taking the training course was to learn more about turbine engines; he had already hot-started this one once and had to replace the hot section as a result.

Later, he had landed the accident airplane gear-up after a go-around on an instrument approach. Requested by the FAA to take a "competency re-examination," the pilot had failed three in a row. The FAA therefore decided that he "lacked the qualifications to be the holder of a Private Pilot Certificate." Slightly more than a year after the gear-up landing, however, he took a fourth re-examination and passed.

Three weeks later, after making a night landing, the pilot taxied off the active runway, only to find himself in the grass. He then reversed direction and taxied back onto the active runway without notifying the tower of his intention. As a result, a 737 on short final had to go around.

The FAA now demanded that he be re-examined again, and also that he undergo "neuropsychological testing" in order to determine whether he was in fact "qualified to hold any class medical certificate." The nature of this testing was left up to the pilot; until it was accomplished, however, he was to abstain from flying. The results of the tests were sent to the FAA Aeromedical Certification Division about six months after the runway incident. He had managed a successful re-examination two days earlier, and received a new temporary certificate.

About five weeks later, someone wrote on an Aeromedical Certification Division staff comments sheet, "Psychology report recently received...does not indicate pathology." The entry was dated, by an odd coincidence, on the very day of the accident that took the lives of the pilot and his three companions.

Two pilots, two airplanes, the same fate. What did they have in common? The King Air pilot was a professional conducting an air taxi operation; the A36 pilot was, literally, a doctor in a Bonanza. Both airplanes were capable and well-equipped. If there was a common element, it was weather of which the pilots were unaware. The pilot of the A36 had not received the AIRMET regarding icing along his route; the pilot of the King Air had not made use of available ground radar services or pilot reports. And there was another similarity: both pilots overstressed their airplanes while trying to recover from dives at speeds far above the designed operating speeds.

An airplane trimmed for cruise cannot gain 100 knots unless it first banks steeply or rolls inverted. If it returns to something like an upright attitude at a very high speed, however, its natural stability applies a considerable tail force to bring it back to its trimmed speed. (Imagine trimming for 160 kias, pushing forward to 240, and then releasing the yoke.) For the pilot to apply enough additional force to overstress the tail is not so difficult as you would imagine. The recovery from a high-speed dive must be made gently, possibly even with initial *forward* pressure on the yoke, and with the help of all the tools available for slowing the airplane down, including the landing gear — limit speeds mean nothing in this kind of emergency — and the propeller, which produces the

most drag when in flat pitch. It is possible to slow an
airplane down from its maximum diving speed without
tearing it apart — but it takes more knowledge and a
cooler head than most pilots who've lost control in the
soup possess.

Out of the Frying Pan

For pilots who regularly fly conventional airplanes for business or travel, the world of ultralights is as remote as those of submarines or skateboards. Ultralights are airplanes intended for recreational use, and limited in gross weight to 254 pounds and in speed to 55 knots. A taxonomist studying their ancestry would probably conclude that they are descendants not of airplanes but of hang gliders; the single thing about them that best defines the place they occupy in the aeronautical world is that a pilot's license is not required to operate them.

Between this Paleozoic level of the aeronautical world and that of the Private Pilot's License is another stratum, termed "recreational." Recreational pilots must have a license. Its requirements are less strict than those of the Private, and the privileges it confers are fewer.

Nevertheless, recreational pilots may operate aircraft of up to four seats and 180 horsepower.

Recreational and ultralight aircraft — the two categories blend somewhat in practice, because airplanes are not constantly being weighed, nor is FAA enforcement around recreational flying very intense — come in a great variety of types. Structurally, many of them have more in common with the tube-and-rag airplanes of the Piper Cub era than with most metal and composite general aviation airplanes of today. The emphasis in their design is on simplicity, maintainability, and low cost.

A fair number of them — what fraction of the fleet, I don't know — incorporate parachutes whose function is to lower not just the occupant(s) but the entire aircraft more or less gently to the ground in an emergency. These are generically known as "Ballistic Recovery Systems" — BRS for short — after the Minnesota company that pioneered them. Chutes were supplied as standard equipment on a certified airplane for the first time in the Cirrus SR-20.Until then, BRS's bread and butter had been the recreational market. The company points to a long list of "saves" that it attributes to its parachutes. From August 1983 to January 2000, it counts 132 lives saved with 112 deployments. The altitude of the highest successful deployment, attributed to an upset in turbulence (which BRS calls "Violent Air"), was at 11,500 feet; the lowest at a somewhat implausible 25 feet. Most were below 1,000 feet; ultralights and recreational aircraft tend to operate at rather low altitudes. The most common reasons for deployment are structural or engine failure and loss of control.

Inevitably, some deployments are unsuccessful. One, which occurred on July 4, 1993, involved a RANS S-12 Airaile. This is a two-seat side-by-side airplane with a pusher engine, typically a Rotax of anywhere from 52 to 100 horsepower. (I suppose an Airaile is some sort of og.)

The pilot was flying on a day of high winds. The wing loading of the RANS is six to seven pounds per square foot of wing area, depending on the engine type; airplanes this lightly loaded are very responsive to gusts and difficult to control in rough air. Witnesses on the ground reported that after "having some difficulty with controllability due to the high winds" the airplane appeared to stall; it spun several turns before hitting the ground. The pilot deployed the BRS, which failed to inflate because it became tangled in the propeller; he died in the crash.

The parachute installation had been "approved" by a technician of the parachute manufacturer on the basis of photographs. The manufacturer required this inspection, but such an approval is self-evidently not to be confused with the "approval" of FAA certification; it merely meant that the technician did not spot any egregious errors. Furthermore, the manufacturer placed significant restrictions on the use of the BRS. Because the chute was in front of the propeller, the engine had to be stopped before it could be deployed. It should not be deployed in "strong winds or convection." Considering that many emergencies seem to take place at low altitude and many deployments must be motivated by an extremity of fright, it could be unrealistic to expect that such limitations would always be remembered or observed.

The National Transportation Safety Board decided that the "probable cause" of the accident was "[t]he inadvertent stall of the airplane." As "factors related to this accident" it listed "...the emergency parachute system that was deployed by the pilot, the partial failure of the parachute survival equipment to deploy properly, and the insufficient information provided by the aircraft parachute manufacturer."

While the NTSB did not characterize the parachute manufacturer as a "cause" but merely as a "related factor," the implication seemed to be that in the NTSB's view the parachute had not come through in the crunch, and therefore was at least slightly blameworthy. Undoubtedly the manufacturer did not agree; after all, the operating limitations for the chute had been violated; why should it be expected to work? Besides, even before the parachute came, or failed to come, into play, the pilot had made a decision to place the airplane and himself at risk.

The notion of an all-forgiving airplane-saver that will lower you to the ground no matter what mistakes you make is at variance with one of the basic tenets of the pilot's creed, namely that flying is a life-and-death activity in which mature judgment and a profound sense of responsibility are fundamental requisites for long survival. (In the short term, good luck is sufficient.) I wonder whether one of the effects of having a parachute aboard might be to tip the scales in favor of trying some impromptu aerobatics, or going up when one might be better advised to stay down; or whether it might encourage a certain sort of pilot to defer needed maintenance. We'll never know whether parachutes actually embolden pilots, or how many deployments would have been avoided if pilots had simply made more cautious decisions.

If one can trust the BRS "saves" list, however, parachutes seem to have been a great boon to recreational aviation. The number of losses of control and structural failures is astonishing — and those are only the airplanes that happened to have parachutes. Either many recreational airplanes must be very poorly made or maintained, or many of their pilots are very inept. Come to think of it, perhaps that's why pilot training, pilot's licenses, and airframe and engine certification were invented in the first place.

Mistaken Identity

It's happened long ago, but the accident remains a
shining example of a confluence of unlikely
circumstances causing a catastrophe when none of them,
by itself, would amount to more than a nuisance.

Five airplanes belonging to Pan Am International Flight
Academy were flying from Deer Valley Airport in
Phoenix to the Palomar Airport at Carlsbad, California
on a May evening in 2004. They left Deer Valley at
intervals of five to 10 minutes. The fourth in the line was
a Piper Seminole, N304PA, flown by two private pilots
who had recently acquired their multi-engine and
instrument ratings. It was a time-building flight for them;
the left-seat pilot had about 175 hours, the other 240.

They filed IFR. Apparently neither had logged any prior
actual instrument experience, but each had around 50

hours of in-flight hood instrument time. They also had, between them, some 50 hours of night flying experience. This would be a significant milestone: a night flight in the air traffic control system with an ILS approach at the destination. It was exactly the kind of straightforward flight — 2 hours, VMC en route, an approach well above minimums at the end — that instrument novices are advised to take.

A few minutes ahead of them in line was another Seminole, N434PA.

Their routing took them south of a couple of big restricted areas and MOAs, along the Mexican border, and over a mountain range, the Volcan, which separates the inland desert from the coastal foothills. On a ridge of the Volcan, at 5,580 feet, is the Julian VOR, which is the initial approach fix for the ILS approach to Palomar.

In was already dark and moonless when, at 2043:48, N304PA contacted the San Diego North Radar sector of Los Angeles Center, reporting level at 8,000. The controller replied with an instruction to fly a heading of 260 after Julian to intercept the Palomar localizer. Two minutes later, the controller instructed N434PA, the Seminole ahead of 304PA, to descend to 6,000, and the crew acknowledged.

Two minutes after that, the controller said, "Seminole 4PA, descend and maintain 5,200." N304PA responded, "Down to 5,200 for 304PA." The controller, whose intent had been that 434PA continue its descent past 6,000 feet, did not notice that the response came from a different call sign. The crew of 434PA was aware of the ambiguity, however, and requested a clarification; but the first part of their transmission was blocked by the controller's instruction to another aircraft. The controller heard only "...for 434PA?" and, possibly thinking the question referred to the transmission he had just made, he replied "No."

At 2049:55, 304PA advised the controller that they had the ATIS for Palomar, and he thanked them. At that point, the Seminole was descending through 6,600, still southeast of the Julian VOR. At 2050:27, the controller, probably noticing that 434PA was approaching the ILS and was still at 6,000, again cleared them to descend to 5,200. 434PA acknowledged, and the controller cleared the flight for the ILS approach to Palomar.

At about the same time, N304PA, in a cruising descent, slammed into the ridge 200 yards from the Julian VOR and about 40 feet below it.

Within a minute, a strong ELT signal was received from the vicinity of the VOR and reported to Center, and at 2053:23 the north sector controller transmitted, "Seminole 4PA, can you come up on 121.5 and check for an ELT please?" He tried eight times to contact N304PA, but there was only silence.

After the third attempt, the controller asked 434PA for a radio check. "5 by 5" was the answer, and the controller then told 434PA to contact Palomar tower. Several minutes later another aircraft transmitted, "SoCal, 6ZP, just for my own heart, did you get a hold of that Seminole?" The controller replied, "No, we're checking right now, I don't — we don't know where it is right now, last we saw of him he was just 5 southeast of Julian same route that you were 4PA."

There had been a perfect storm of verbal confusion. The controller, probably rattled and fearing that the ELT might be from an airplane that he had been working, was still using the ambiguous call sign "4PA", and was seemingly confusing 6ZP with 434PA, which he himself had sent off the frequency several minutes earlier. It is not clear from the NTSB report whether the controller, working two airplanes on identical flight plans, separated from one another by a few minutes and at most 25 miles, ever reflected that using an abbreviated call sign set the stage for confusion between them. The crew of 434PA at least seems to have felt a momentary uncertainty; it was only by a piece of extraordinarily bad luck that their query to the controller, which might have clarified the whole situation, was blocked in such a way that the controller's irrelevant reply seemed appropriate to the crew's question.

The MEA for the airway segment approaching Julian from the southeast is 7,700 feet, and for the initial portion of the transition from Julian to the Palomar ILS it is 6,800 feet. Los Angeles Center had two separate systems for detecting and issuing alerts about minimum safe altitude violations. One, which used a radar located at the 6,200-foot level on a mountaintop 18 miles southeast of Julian, provided uninterrupted coverage of the airway along which N304PA approached the VOR. That system was in use by the Center Sector 9 controller who had handed off 304PA to San Diego North at 2043. It had continued to display the flight's data block until the controller forced it off his display about a minute before the accident. As N304PA descended below 7,800 feet — approximately a minute after receiving an instruction for "4PA" that was actually intended for the airplane ahead of it — a Minimum Safe Altitude Warning (MSAW) alert was presented to the Sector 9 controller. He ignored it, presumably thinking that the San Diego North controller, who then had responsibility for the airplane, would deal with it.

The altitude warning system used by the San Diego North controller relied on a different radar, however, this one located near the coast at the Miramar Naval Air Station. It provided imperfect coverage of aircraft flying low over the mountains. Nevertheless, it detected N304PA about a minute before the crash, sounded an alert to the controller, and placed a flashing red "LA" (low altitude) warning above the descending Seminole's data block. The flashing warning remained for only a few seconds, however, before the airplane sank out of view behind the ridge, the radar track went into "coast" status, and the alert terminated. The NTSB report on the accident does not explain why the controller did not respond to the MSAW alert or why he apparently failed to connect it with the subsequent ELT signal.

The NTSB cited two causes and one contributing factor in its accident report. The causes were, first, the San Diego North controller's "incorrect use of an abbreviated callsign" and his failure to notice that the readback used a callsign different from that of the intended recipient of the clearance; and second, "the pilots' failure to question a clearance that descended them below the published [MEA]." The contributing factor was the failure of both Center and TRACON controllers to "properly respond" to the MSAW alerts.

It is difficult to imagine that during the earlier course of the flight, prior to the handoff to San Diego TRACON, the similarity between the call signs of the two Seminoles went unnoticed by any of the pilots or controllers. Perhaps the pilots were aware of it; they seem, at least in all of the transmissions quoted in the NTSB's report, always to have used their full call signs. It's even possible that the subject was discussed before takeoff. The controller, on the other hand, seems to have made no effort to clearly distinguish between the two airplanes, nor to have been aware of the possibility of a dangerous confusion.

Should the two pilots of N304PA have realized that they were descending below the MEA? They should; but they were inexperienced and perhaps still believed in the infallibility of controllers, and so it is not too surprising that they didn't. While pilots on IFR flight plans can't be expected to track their progress on VFR charts, they should still be aware of the general nature of the terrain below them and along the route ahead, and anticipate likely altitude changes before they occur. MEAs are MEAs; a descent that violates an MEA at least merits a question. There is always a possibility of a faulty or misunderstood clearance. Everyone makes mistakes; but the ground is always right.

We're On Fire!

On a Sunday afternoon in September, 2009, a Piper Saratoga with four aboard was approaching Fort Lauderdale on an IFR flight plan from Gainesville. The weather was fine, with scattered clouds and mild winds. The airplane was at 3,800 feet on a heading of about 145 degrees, and was being handled by a Miami (MIA) approach controller.

Then — "Mayday mayday mayday mayday! 2467Y has a fire in the engine."

Time 1745:55

MIA — N2467Y Miami, roger, are you going to try and make it to Executive Airport — that's the closest airport to you sir.

67Y — We're trying … we got smoke in the cockpit and we're trying to get to the … nearest airport.

MIA — N2767Y [sic] roger fly heading of 110, proceed direct to Executive Airport, that's the closest airport actually to you.

67Y — 110 on the heading, 67Y.

Time 1746:24

MIA — N67Y the Pahokee airport is actually the closest airport to you, it is 23.93 miles away, do you want to try and get to Pahokee or do you want to get to Exec?

67Y — We'd like to get to Exec. I think what we did is we, we definitely got, we were able, we have power, I think we've lost one … cylinder or something like that, we can see some fire coming off the nose the smoke in the cockpit has dissipated, we can maintain altitude, ah, will just have to keep you posted …

Time 1747:02

MIA — N67Y you wanna still try to make Fort Lauderdale Exec, that is, it is 24 miles away, is that, that's the … do you want to try to continue to Exec, correct?

67Y — We're gonna try and continue to Exec, 67Y.

MIA — N67Y, keep me advised, sir.

67Y — Will do, 67Y.

Time 1747:50

67Y — Ah, we want visual straight in to the runway, 67Y.

MIA — N2467Y, fly heading 110, that'll be vectors straight in to Executive Runway 8 at Executive for visual approach ... N2467Y proceed heading 110, that'll take you direct to Exec for a visual approach Runway 8.

67Y — 110, 67Y, visual eight.

MIA — N2467Y I'm keep you at altitude just so you can stay up there hopefully if you have another problem you can glide to the airport but I will keep you at 3,000, advise me if you want to do anything other than that.

67Y — Thank you very much, 67Y.

At this point, the Miami controller gave 67Y a new frequency, so that a Fort Lauderdale (FXE) approach controller could handle him alone. The pilot came up on the new frequency.

Time 1749:40

FXE — N67Y, I understand you have heading, like I say we also have Boca, Boca is about the same distance, so whichever one you look like 12 o'clock and 25 miles for Executive.

67Y — We're getting more smoke in the cockpit, we're thinking we might have to land on runway .. ah highway 27 here.

FXE — Okay, do you have 27 ... You said you wanna try and land on Highway 27, sir?

67Y — Yes yes

FXE — All right 67Y we have your ... can I get the souls on board and fuel?

Time 1750:14

FXE — 67Y, before, can you give me the souls on board please?

Time 1750:28

FXE — N2467Y, can you give me souls on board?

67Y — We're on fire! We're on fire!

A Florida Wildlife Conservation officer saw the Saratoga in a steep left bank, diving, trailing black smoke, with flames pouring from the cowling. It crashed at high speed into six feet of water, killing all aboard.

At the time of the original mayday call, the Saratoga was about four miles west of Highway 27 — a wide, straight road free of railings and power lines — and flying exactly parallel to it. It was 22 nm from both Clewiston and Pahokee airports, and about 16 nm from Belle Glade State. Fort Lauderdale Executive, which the controller initially told the pilot was the nearest airport, was 34 nm distant. At 1747, when the controller told the pilot that Exec was 24 miles away, it was actually still more than 30 miles away.

The airplane was pulverized, but investigators were able to localize the source of the fire at the number 5 cylinder — right rear on a Lycoming — and, through electron microscopy, to identify a fatigue fracture on a fuel line just above that cylinder's injector. The breaking of the fuel supply line was the primary probable cause. "Also causal," the report continues, "was the pilot's failure to immediately secure the engine/perform a forced landing after discovery of the fire, which resulted in the pilot's loss of control of the airplane."

The key thing to understand about an engine fire is that there is very little in the engine compartment that can burn, other than the fuel being fed to the engine and the oil circulating through it. The emergency procedure for an engine fire is easy to remember. It consists of two steps: Shut off fuel (first idle cutoff, then tank selector valve to off, while leaving the mags on), then land. The concern is to save lives, not the airplane. Of course, some judgment is still needed; you don't want to shut down the engine where there is no possibility of a survivable landing, but you don't want to keep it running while you hunt for a more agreeable place to spent the night.

There are some refinements. For example, if what is burning is oil, signaled by dense black or gray smoke, it is desirable to stop the prop (coarse pitch, closed throttle, slow down) to eliminate oil pressure. If flames are coming from the cowling, a slip can be used to keep them away from the cabin. A high gliding speed and open cowl flaps may "blow the fire out" by leaning remaining fuel or oil vapors to an incombustible mixture.

But the most important thing is to get onto the ground. The same applies to a twin, even though it seems able to keep flying. Once a fire has begun, it is impossible to know what is going on inside a cowling and whether a wing or engine mount has been weakened.

Probably many pilots, after once reading the "Engine Fire" section of the POH, gradually forget it. The Saratoga's was emphatic: first shut off the fuel supply to the engine. It's logical. If your house were on fire, would you squirt gasoline on it? Of course, the signs can be ambiguous. Oil dripping on an exhaust pipe or turbocharger can produce a burning odor and copious smoke, without a flame. But in this case there was no ambiguity: They saw flames.

Why didn't the pilot land immediately?

It's not hard to put yourself into his place. The Florida
Everglades are open, flat and shallow, but not an inviting
place to spend the night. He cannot have been unaware of
the nearby highway, but it was a Sunday afternoon, when
the yearning to get back is at its peak. The home airport
was almost in sight, and it had fire fighting equipment.
The smoke in the cockpit had subsided, giving hope that
the worst was over. And then there is the bane of pilots:
irrational optimism, the feeling that this cannot happen to
me.

It is worth reflecting, parenthetically, on the role of
controllers. They appear to most pilots as authority
figures. The Miami controller's first reaction to the pilot's
mayday call was, "Are you going to try and make it to
Executive Airport?" Compared with the neutral "Say
your intentions," this was a leading question. "Do you
intend to make a precautionary landing?" would have
pointed in a different direction. Perhaps from a
misguided impulse to provide encouragement, he
identified Executive as the nearest airport; it was not, by
a factor of two. Later, he said he would "keep" the flight
at 3,000 feet, whereas what it really needed to do was get
down as quickly as possible. At 1747:02, he told the pilot
it was 24 miles to the airport; more than two and a half
minutes later, the second controller said he was 25 miles
out.

It is must be painful to decide to crash-land a beloved airplane, especially when hope obscures the grim consequences of not doing so. But an in-flight fire is a terrible thing: It leaves no choice.

232

Or Not To Be

Suicide is the official probable cause of perhaps two accidents a year. It is also implicated, but not blamed, in a few unexplained collisions with terrain involving pilots with histories of depression or previous suicide attempts, but who did not leave notes or otherwise express an intention to take their lives.

The desire to spend one's last hours flying is one with which at least some pilots will sympathize. The desire to end one's flying career with a crash, on the other hand, may be more difficult to comprehend. But there is a practical aspect: from flight to death, once you turn in that direction, is not very far.

There must be as many motives — rage, despondency, depression, shame — as there are suicidal pilots. Some end their lives with a kamikaze attack on their own home or an estranged wife or girlfriend's. (In the past 15 years all the pilots who have committed suicide by flying into buildings have been men.) One man, for example, abruptly quit his job and left home. He returned to the house a week later to leave a suicide note, apparently with the intention of discomfiting his wife. Three days later, he took off in a Cherokee Arrow and flew the tanks almost empty — he was airborne for five hours and 20 minutes — before diving into his house. Since there was no fuel left to speak of, there was no fire. Another man, having been barred from his residence by a court restraining order, came back home in his Trinidad. Another man crashed his airplane beside a church in which a woman who had declined his proposal of marriage was attending a service.

In a variation upon this theme, another pilot, who crashed a Cessna 120 into a forest, first shot his wife, who was in the right seat. Ten days after the accident they were found, her body still in her seat, his beside the airplane. The medical examiner attributed his death to "acute ethanol intoxication," a conclusion that implies, perhaps unintentionally, a bizarre scenario: he survived the accident and then drank himself to death.

A number of suicides were associated with legal troubles. One pilot, who had been charged with "lewd and lascivious conduct with a minor," fell to drinking heavily and spoke of intentionally crashing his Malibu. The next day he did just that, while in radio communication with approach control. He reported descending through

11,000 feet, then through 6,000 just 38 seconds later. He reached the ground at 4,650.

Another pilot, having been found guilty for the second time of running an illegal pyramid scheme, and apprehensive about the possibility of being sentenced to jail, flew a rented 152 straight into a mountain.

Another, a TV weather presenter whose alleged extramarital affair and harassment of a woman had been the subject of local new reports, told coworkers that he had attempted suicide twice in recent days, once in an airplane. He then took off in an Archer and plunged vertically into the runway at full power.

A pilot who was both a minister and an insurance agent, and who had owned a 1960 Bonanza for two years, was indicted for felony theft in connection with his insurance business. Released on bail, he wrote e-mails to several members of his congregation begging their forgiveness and then departed in his Bonanza, which crashed in level high desert terrain. The coroner ruled the death a suicide, but the National Transportation Safety Board confined itself to "controlled descent into terrain for reasons undetermined."

Another subject of a criminal investigation told numerous friends that he would kill himself by intentionally crashing an airplane before he would go to jail. True to his word, he rented a 152, sat in it for half an hour prior to taking off, and then departed never to return.

Another, who had a history of drug use and had been previously convicted of an arson, was being sought by police in connection with another arson. Having left behind a power of attorney for his brother, he rented an airplane, buzzed a number of boats, and then crashed into the ocean. The airplane sank, but the pilot's floating body was recovered and tested positive for alcohol, cocaine, and Valium.

Feelings of despair or grief drove others to a fatal flight. A pilot whose wife had left him the day before dove into terrain after leaving on an answering machine a message desiring to "see my son ... one more time." The pilot had methodically collected the titles to the family vehicles, signed and notarized them, and left them for his wife. Another, despondent over the death of his mother and concerned that he might lose his FAA medical because of his deteriorating heart condition, wrote out a will leaving his new sports car to his girlfriend, rented a 172, flew out over the ocean, did a loop — perhaps something he had always wanted to do in a 172 — and plunged into the water.

Some pilots seem to call for help at the same time as they pass beyond it. One made a distress call saying that he was "going in" before flying into a cliff in VFR weather. By way of explaining himself, he had left his autobiography, his medical history, and his wife's death

certificate in his parked car. Another changed his
transponder squawk to 7700, the emergency code, before
flying straight and level into a mountain. Another, who
also squawked 7700 and transmitted a distress call saying
that his airplane had fuel pressure problems, then
parachuted from his airplane, of which he was the only
occupant. He did not survive the jump, but it was almost
a year before his body was found. The NTSB's oddly-
phrased probable cause was "the pilot's intentional
decision to abandon the airplane and allow it to fly
unattended," but the accident report noted that the pilot
had earlier left his wife a message saying, "I don't want
to live any more."

Some pilots have engaged in poignantly ambiguous
dialogues with controllers. One took off at night in a 182
and climbed past 21,000 feet before establishing radio
contact with a controller. He reported that he was out of
fuel. The controller directed him to an airport, but the
pilot remarked, "Yeah, I prefer water." As he glided
down, the pilot, whose use of language is endearing,
continued to speak of a water landing; "All things
considered," he said, "I think that would be the best place
to go." At another point he said, "As you might have
guessed, I have not had a good day … I'm going
swimming tonight." Indeed, he had not had a good day;
the night before he had been involved in a fatal hit-and-
run accident, and there was a warrant out for his arrest.
He crashed in darkness into a frozen reservoir.

Another pilot was doing touch-and-gos in a Seminole when he suddenly asked the tower controller to copy down a phone number. "You don't need to use it...yet," he said. "It looks like one more option and then a full stop." He flew another circuit, then asked the controller to call the number and "let them know where I'm at, also, if you could, tell my family and friends that I love them very much."

"Were you going to depart out of here or stay the night?" the controller asked, still unaware of the double meaning of the conversation.

"I'll stay the night," the pilot said, and added a few seconds later, "It would be a good idea to get airport rescue and fire fighting out here too please."

"Are you declaring an emergency?" the controller asked.

There was no reply. The airplane made a low approach, increased speed, pulled nearly straight up, stalled at 1,000 feet, and crashed on the runway.

A more laconic pilot, also in a Seminole, having left a note saying "I do not want to live," approached his home runway very high. The tower controller asked whether he would be able to get down and land, and the pilot replied "This will be my final landing." He pushed the nose over, increased power, and dived into the runway.

The most famous suicide flights in recent memory were those of September 11th 2001. Their motive, of course, was not personal extinction, but a political and religious mission. The horrifying possibility that at the controls of a commercial airliner could sit a pilot bent on self-destruction had been strangely foreshadowed three years earlier, when the first officer of an EgyptAir flight from New York to Cairo dove the Boeing 767 into the Atlantic south of Nantucket, taking 216 other souls with him. His motive has never been known, and the Egyptian government, vigorously denying that the crash had been a deliberate act at all, issued its own report, blaming alleged defects in the control system of the 767. The cockpit voice recorder tape, however, was scarcely consistent with the theory that the first officer was trying to save rather than destroy the airplane. The bureaucratic dispute, like the first officer's incessant repetition of an Arabic phrase, translated as "I rely on God," left many Americans ominously bewildered. Yet the mystery of that crash was, in a way, not so different from those of other suicide flights. All death-bent pilots seem, when the wheels leave the ground on their final flights, already to have passed over into a foreign land at whose language and customs we who have not visited it can only guess.

Glossary

A&P airframe and powerplant mechanic

AD notice Airworthiness Directive, a notification to pilots from the FAA of some problem or defect in their airplanes that needs to be corrected, often at considerable cost

ADF a direction-finding navigational radio whose display contains an arrow that points toward the transmitter to which it is tuned

agl above ground level

AIRMET a message disseminated to pilots to warn of weather conditions that might affect safety of flight. The most ominous warnings are called SIGMETs.

ATIS Automated Terminal Information Service, a recorded announcement of airport conditions, available by radio or telephone

ATC Air Traffic Control

ATP Air Transport Pilot, the highest level of pilot license

block altitude a range of protected altitudes issued to a pilot by a controller, eg 2,000 to 4,000 feet, as opposed to a single assigned altitude

Center any en route air traffic control facility

Class B controlled airspace surrounding a major airport

circling approach an instrument approach procedure that is not aligned with the runway

CFII Certified Flight Instructor, Instrument

CVR Cockpit Voice Recorder

DUAT an online and telephone weather briefing service for pilots

EAA Experimental Aircraft Association

EFIS Electronic Flight Instrumentation System, a "glass panel" in which information is presented to the pilot electronically rather than with the traditional round mechanical instruments

ELT Emergency Locator Transmitter, a transmitter triggered by a sudden shock or deceleration, intended to guide rescuers to a crash site.

empennage the tail surfaces of an airplane

FAA Federal Aviation Administration, the branch of the Department of Transportation that regulates aviation

FAR Federal Aviation Regulations

FL Flight Level, a convention for reporting altitude at or above 18,000 feet. The letters are followed by the altitude in hundreds of feet; thus, FL 250 is 25,000 feet.

fpm feet per minute, used for rates of climb or descent

FSS Flight Service Station, a source of flight planning information and other services for pilots

GPS Global Positioning System, satellite-based navigation similar to the systems found in cars

IFR Instrument Flight Rules, a set of rules and procedures used when flying blind -- although many flights, including all airline flights, are conducted under IFR even in clear weather

ILS Instrument Landing System — the standard type of runway approach, providing both lateral (localizer) and vertical (glideslope) guidance

IMC Instrument Meteorological Conditions — basically, clouds

242

intersection a navigational fix defined as the intersection of two radial beams from different transmitting locations

kias, ktas knots indicated or true airspeed. At altitude, reduced air density makes the airspeed indicator show a speed lower than the true one.

knot a unit of speed, used in aviation for no good reason, equal to 1.15 mph

lenticular, rotor a lenticular cloud is a smooth, lens-shaped cloud that appears when strong winds below over mountain ridges; beneath the lenticular there is likely to be a region of extreme turbulence called a rotor

limit load factor the highest G load an airplane will sustain without permanent deformation

localizer a radio beam providing lateral, but not vertical, guidance to a runway

MDA Minimum Descent Altitude, the lowest a plane can legally go on an instrument approach if the pilot cannot see the runway

MEA Minimum Enroute Altitude for IFR aircraft along a given route segment

MOA Military Operations Area

Mode C the altitude-reporting function of an airplane's radar transponder

navcom navigation/communication radio

NOTAM a federally-generated Notice to Airmen regarding things like facilities that are temporarily out of service

nm nautical mile, 1.15 statute miles

o'clock direction expressed as a clock face with the pilot facing 12.

Part 135 regulations regarding commuter and air taxi services

PFD Primary Flight Display

POH Pilot's Operating Handbook, the information manual for a particular airplane type

primary echoes radar returns from surface of the airplane itself as opposed to its transponder

SIGMET a message disseminated to pilots to warn of a potentially dangerous weather condition

SMEL a pilot rating for single- and multi-engine landplanes

stepdown approach an instrument approach in which permissible altitude decreases in a series of steps rather than a constant slope

Stormscope an onboard thunderstorm-detection device that depends on lightning rather than radar reflectivity

squawk the reply sent by an airplane's transponder to a radar interrogation from the ground

TRACON a local or regional air traffic control center

transponder a device that replies to radar interrogations from ground stations

Unicom a radio frequency used at some airports, especially uncontrolled ones, for advisory services

vector an instruction, given by a controller to a pilot, to fly in a certain direction

VFR Visual Flight Rules, a set of rules governing flight in visual conditions, as opposed to IFR, Instrument Flight Rules, for flying blind

VMC Visual Meteorological Conditions — weather good enough to allow a pilot to see and avoid obstacles and traffic

VOR a type of radio-beam navigation system